SUN TZU

FOR THE

DIGITAL AGE

the BUSINESS person's step-by-step guide to DOMINATE and INFLUENCE your industry, WIN online customers, and EARN with social sales

THE UNCUT VERSION

PHOENIX SHELDON-BAKER

a self-published book

Self-Published by Phoenix Sheldon-Baker

Printed by CreateSpace, an Amazon.com Company, Charleston SC.
www.createspace.com

Copyright © Phoenix Sheldon-Baker 2017. *All Rights Reserved*

First Published 2017
First Edition 2017

Cover Illustration: Shutterstock Image

Copyright subsists in this work. No part of this work may be reproduced, stored in a retrieval system or transmitted in any form or by any means without the prior written permission of the author or publisher, except by a reviewer who may quote passages in a reference. Any unauthorized reproduction of this work will constitute a copyright infringement and render the doer liable under both civil and criminal law.

Whilst every effort has been made to ensure the information published in this work is accurate, the editor, author, writer, contributor, publisher and printer takes no responsibility for any loss or damage suffered by any person as a result of the reliance upon the information contained herein.

ISBN-13: 978-1539452683   (print)
ISBN-10: 1539452689   (ePub)

all feedback welcomed on thephoenix@execs.com

SUN TZU FOR THE DIGITAL AGE

Introduction	1
STRATEGIC ASSESSMENTS	**5**
WHY YOU NEED STRATEGY	7
COMPILE A STRATEGIC ASSESSMENT	12
PROFILE YOUR ONLINE CUSTOMER	15
SWOT THE COMPETITION	19
COMPILE A COMPETITOR'S ANALYSIS	26
STEP 1: LOCATE YOUR COMPETITORS ONLINE	28
STEP 2: PREPARE 3 COMPARATIVE GRIDS	28
STEP 3: ADD THE COMPETITORS TO EACH GRID	31
STEP 4: ENTER THE DATA INTO GRID 1	33
STEP 5: ENTER THE DATA INTO GRID 2	37
STEP 6: ENTER THE DATA INTO GRID 3	38
STEP 7: EXAMINE THEIR CONTENT MARKETING STRATEGIES	40
STEP 8: COMPILE YOUR BRANDS' SWOT	44
STEP 9: DETERMINE YOUR MARKET SHARE	47
DOMINATE AND INFLUENCE SYSTEMATICALLY	49
DOING BATTLE	**55**
DEVELOP YOUR POLICY	57
POLICY #1: INVEST RESOURCE TO SUSTAIN YOUR EFFORTS	58
POLICY #2: DO THINGS TIMEOUSLY … AS IN SPEEDILY	61
POLICY #3: STRENGTHEN YOURSELF WITH EACH WIN	65
POLICY #4: KNOW YOUR STUFF	68
LAUNCH STRATEGIC ATTACKS	70
WIN ONLINE CUSTOMERS WITHOUT A FIGHT	70
LEAD YOUR MARKETING AND SALES TEAM	74
RULES OF ENGAGEMENT	**79**
APPLY RULES OF ENGAGEMENT TO SOCIAL SALES	81

SUCCESS BEGINS WITH INTEL	83
MAINTAIN YOUR OBJECTIVES	84
ESTABLISH A SECURE POSITION	86
BE ON AND STAY ON THE OFFENSIVE	88
SURPRISE THEM	89
MANOEUVRE INTO A POSITION OF STRENGTH	90
CONCENTRATE RESOURCES, FOCUS STRENGTHS	91
ECONOMY OF FORCE IS THE GOVERNING PRINCIPLE	91
KEEP IT SIMPLE AND EARN WITH SOCIAL SALES	92
FORMATION	**99**
THE PRIMARY OBJECTIVE IN APPLYING STRATEGY	101
ADAPT TO THE NEW WORLD [WIDE WEB] ORDER	102
INTELLIGENCE	**109**
ROUTINE REPORTING	111
WEBSITE ANALYTICS	113
SOCIAL MEDIA ANALYTICS	118
FACEBOOK	118
TWITTER	124
LINKEDIN	127
ANALYTICS FOR OTHER SOCIAL MEDIA PLATFORMS	131
Conclusion	133
Sources	137
Recommended Analytic Platforms	138
Links for Further Information	139

"Every battle is won before it is fought"
Sun Tzu

Sun Tzu
544 BC – 496 BC

Victory is reserved for those who are willing to pay its price

*Strategy without tactics is the slowest route to victory.
Tactics without strategy is the noise before defeat.*

*The General who wins the battle makes many calculations in his
Temple before the battle is fought*

INTRODUCTION

THIS BOOK IS THE UNCUT VERSION AND CONTAINS EXPLICIT, PROFANE AND OFFENSIVE LANGUAGE, WRITTEN TO SIMULATE THE INDUCTION LANGUAGE OF ANY TRAINING REGIMEN FOR THOSE PREPARING TO GO TO WAR. IF YOU ARE SQUEAMISH OR CRINGE AT THE USE OF WORDS SUCH AS FUCK AND SHIT, THEN RATHER GET THE CUT VERSION OF THIS BOOK.

Your business NEEDS a powerful war strategy for the marketplace so you can dominate your online space and reap the benefits of wealth.

Here's a secret – your business, the way it is now, can make literally billions – you just need an actionable strategy to get it there. The biggest businesses in the world have risen to the top in time, backed with several excellent strategies. We're not just talking marketing strategy here – if you're a business owner, a C-Suite exec ... hell, yeah, even a management consultant wanting to advise your client to get them to the top ... best you read this book.

This book is for winners, and for people who have chosen to succeed at all costs. Why do I say that? Sun Tzu wrote The Art of War, an ancient Chinese treatise on war strategy. This script has the answers to conquer any army, any order, any so-called power. When you apply Sun Tzu's strategic principles, you are able to rise to greatness.

You see, you may have succumbed somewhere in the business environment to some pecking order of those who are just doing it right, well kind of anyway. And in your digital dealings, you're telling yourself … it's recession, its budget; it's the lack of talent, its … blah-blah-blah. Dude, babe, just cut it out right now. Excuses are not going to get you there. Let's call things the way they are. You've been burned man! Your company is on fire! It's collapsing without the right strategy! Reality factor needs to kick in. Or maybe It's making money, fine … but it's going backwards like a receding tide. You get it? You've been on social media and had a website for the past what? 10, 15 years or so, and always asking yourself why nothing you do online seems to work. You're covered in ash, and all you now have left, really, is a heartbeat.

This book, will dust those ashes off, and renew your vigor to flap your wings and fly again – and this time, way above the sun, man. So many people are going to benefit from this when you do it. Got it? Do it, just fucken do it!

My name is Phoenix. I'm a specialist in strategy. And that's not just because I was the top student in the country or any of those other laurels to brag about. I have experience in steering and interfacing with F500 companies at board level to get them to position themselves where they need to be. But hey, more about that later – this book is not about me, it's about you, your business and what you're doing to position your biz to own your space in income, dominance and influence.

Tracking with me?

Ok, strategy. So, I'm talking about hard truths here. The economy is where the war is at. It's not where the weapons of mass destruction and nukes and tanks and Muslims chopping Christian's heads off are at. It's far worse than that. You see, your business *makes* the economy. And it's very cutthroat. It's as good as them chopping your head off if you don't make it. It's a cruel universe out there and only the strongest are surviving. You're going to lead or be led. You're going to dominate your sphere or be eaten alive … left to starve to death, along with all your dependents. Are you actually equipped to fight the good fight, dude? I mean, really, think about it. Are you able to fight for business and get income surging through your corporate veins and bank account?

I got the answers you're looking for right here, in this book. Ready to wage war and claim back your survival? Are you ready to put all the shit behind you? Just like, fucking let it go man! You're going to get real busy with the pages that follow, because this is your blue print to digital success. I'm here to help you. I'm here to see you succeed. I'm here to give you tools to break through every fucken barrier holding you back from reaching greatness and wealth, and show you how to work these tools.

And it all starts with … strategy.

Ready?

Turn the page.

PART 1

STRATEGIC ASSESSMENTS

Why You Need Strategy

The first rule about strategy is SIMPLICITY.

That's right – Sun Tzu wrote about The Art of War. War is quite simple when you reduce it to its basic concepts. It's essentially involving large bodies of troops armed with personal weapons, and in Sun Tzu's time – like almost 3,000 years ago – was really about land battles. So, let's draw an analogy right here ok, about how this all relates to social media and digital marketing.

Social media involves many networks, mediums, you know – I mean we all know about Facebook, LinkedIn, Twitter, YouTube, Google Plus right? Those are the big 5. Then we got a whole bunch of apps that can open with any of these – yeah that's right: Instagram, Pinterest, Houseparty, Periscope … blah-blah-blah. Plenty of mediums around. Then using these networks are followers. Ok, call them different things on different networks: fans, friends, connections, igers, whatever. You get the point right. And these characters are linked to you somehow by choice; and you're linked to them as well. How? Your page! It may be by your personal profile, or your company page, or something like that. So, to simplify it all, we got the following things:

Social media networks
Followers
Pages

Let's contextualize this observation because we're talking mainly about business here, right.

So, your Business, your company, *your brand page* is on social media (if not, it should be!), and it has followers, and you're following other categories of people too – other people and businesses and brands.

And that's not all, you have your company website that is like your home, your country, in cyberspace – the domain of the Internet as we know it. And we're not even talking about the deep web here that is like a trillion times bigger than the Internet as most of us know it. But we don't want to go to the deep web – that's your hell, trust me. Internet is heaven compared; let's leave it there.

Your social media is connected (or should at least be via links in your bio and content) to your website, and *vice versa*. If not, again, I can only urge you to get linked as much as possible. So your social media pages are the vehicles you send out into cyberspace to capture market share and to bring customers or prospects back to your website, your castle, your fortress, citadel, to trade. Get where I'm going with this?

Of course, there's other ways people can reach you. They can find you via Google or any of their preferred search engines, click through to your website or social media sites, and see what you got. And that's where your emissaries, your ambassadors play a role – you see somewhere, somehow people, most often strangers, need to get to know *you*, and know where you *are*, what you *got*, what you can *do*, and how your stuff can *benefit* them. And many times, there's much word-of-mouth going on from your brand ambassadors and all your PR channels that get the word out: *hey brand XYZ is in the house*!

So where's the war?

It's all around you man. It's on the Internet. It's a war for followers. It's a war to get those followers to buy from you, and not some other fuck next door. It's a war for their attention, because; let's face it, these followers have like ADHD+ online. They're the most disloyal motherfuckers you've ever met in your life. And they're disloyal for as long as you do not feed them. They're surviving for themselves and its total anarchy out there. They will mute you, block you, and shut you out if unsatisfied. No second chance! You fuck up, you are history, BAM! – and so is your brand!

Sure, you can capture millions of followers online, that's the easy part. And no - they will not ALL buy from you. Yet, being connected to them, you're connected to their peeps, their followers, their networks, and so by a domino order have more reach – so make the impression! (Nice pun, if you're a digital marketer). Yes, its war out there, and your competition is your enemy. They are making bucks – big fucking bucks, while you're getting fucked with spiraling budgets and marketing spend, and useless fucken idiots that call themselves social media managers, community managers and the likes. If you're a social media manager reading this, then don't worry - you're no longer a fucken idiot, simply because you're learning the ropes to win now.

It's a full on war to win influence, loyalty, and customers. Followers are the enemy. That's right, think about it, a treasonous son of a bitch who cannot stick to you or your brand, but will click away and eat in a greener, more convenient pasture elsewhere, this fucker is your enemy! A customer is not your friend – throw that thinking out the fucking window man. It does not cut it in the digital media landscape. Don't get me wrong: I'm not advocating the need to pursue each and every follower and become all desperate for followers. With the right strategy to dominate and influence, you won't have to worry about these things, as they will come to you in droves.

There's a different war to be fought here – it's not about putting a gun to your customers' head and telling them to buy from you, or else! You got to be all-nice with the fucker because your follower has ALL the power man! That's right, they have the power to be disloyal thanks to democracy and freedom of choice. And you're their victim. You need them to spend on you because otherwise you and those that work for you, their families and friends, will not benefit, and you'll all be history!

Can you afford to be done like that?

I did not think so. You're on the board; you're that CEO with some nice lavish lifestyle, you're on the C-Suite, isn't that sweet? Why's your company not a Fortune 500 this year? Ever? And if you're even ranking, why has your position not improved year on year?

I'll tell you why ... you're not fighting enough!

You lazy, ignorant son of a bitch! You're in treason to your entire company right now because you haven't got a strategy executed yet. Sure, you got advisors, and people you pay hefty packages to - for doing what? Those same schmucks are sitting in your boardroom on social media while you blab away about EBITDA, dividends and disbursements, clicking through their networks liking even your competition and buying from them!

This is so ironic. I was at the Toyota plant in Durban South Africa the other day. It was quite shocking to find so many Mercedes and BMW parked in the Executive bays. I asked the security there – whose cars are those man? *Eish Mista*, the chap responded in broken Zulu, *ees da big bosses of da cumpanee!*

Yeah, you mean the execs that sell Toyota drive another brand? Holy fuck! You get my point! What's your strategy man? Your friends and followers *are* your enemies! What you going to do to swing them and get them to bat on the same team man?

Again, it's all in the strategy you use. Ok, I hear you now; you have a strategy that some prick from Deloitte's or PwC, or Accenture popped out for you. Ok. Ok. Great, then let's refine it a bit to Samurai quality, shall we?

What we're essentially pushing for here, is to plan the right strategy before we go and wage war in cyberspace, so that we can avoid casualties to your brand as far as possible – hey, you may be following the wrong peeps, so we'll just have to nuke those at some point, and get the right peeps, right? We're alluding to the tactical base of strategy now. You know, different ways of doing things that will result in what we want at the end of the day. We need to find the right way to do things to get these enemies to obey us.

When we speak about strategy we refer to the general onslaught of our enemies – and these things clearly create the borders – or at least will, if they're not already defined online.

To clarify something quickly here: this is not strategy like you get in politics or the military. Those have their strategic fields defined in terms of geo-strategic factors like state borders and governments. In digital strategy we're dealing with the mental constructs of influence and market share, where there are clear positions or nodes that can be found, like your website and social media platforms.

In short, your strategy stems from your business, and ends at these platforms and domains. Got it? Tactics on the other hand begin with how you engage your enemy – your online customer, and convert them to follow you, refer others to you, buy your stuff, advocate you to their networks, and so on and so forth. So, let's be clear on these terms from the outset as these tend to be used interchangeably.

Strategy and tactics.

Per Sun Tzu, the fundamentals of strategy remain the same and are still applied today. It's only the tactics that change, that we can modify and innovate upon.

An excellent strategy implemented and executed will drive these people to your brand to do business without you having to do too much thereafter; at which point you can say you have won the war. But let's not get ahead of ourselves yet, we got to go through the Sun Tzu teaching to understand more about how it applies to you and your business.

Tell you what, if you implement what I am telling you in this book, and it works for you – which it will, I have no doubt about my product – my product here is practical knowledge which I am giving to you – then why not contact me, and let me sit on your board in some advisory capacity, give me a title if you must, and I will monitor your forward strategy from thereon out. Deal?

And if this book fails for you, contact me; I will assess what you've done and give you a free consultation to get it back on track. But you need to show me you've done something to execute your strategy. And I don't want to hear about budget issues. When you do this right, budget will never be a factor again!

That's the mindset I want to hear.

We're going to war peeps! No time for losers, no time for excuses. Put the battle field in your mind now – it's in cyberspace, your digital online presence is the only thing that can act as a base for attack into the cyber-landscape where we are going to fuck these followers up, and make them slaves, where they can bow to your brand.

Are you ready to make money online? Are you ready to fight for your domain? Are you ready to conquer the hearts and minds of these treacherous followers? Are you going to do this, all or nothing? Are you going to do whatever the fuck it takes to rise from the ashes? Are you feeling motivated and excited yet?

Compile a Strategic Assessment

Sun Tzu's thesis, Art of War, begins pretty much with assessing the situation you find yourself in. Why? Because you need a clear vision where you are headed and what is happening. You need an R-factor, reality check, ok.

Check this out:

> *Sun Tzu says:*
>
> *War is a matter of vital importance to the state; a matter of life and death, the road either to survival or to ruin. Hence it is imperative that it be thoroughly studied.*

Therefore, measure in terms of five things, use these assessments to make comparisons and thus find out what the conditions are. The five things are:

1. *The way*
2. *The weather*
3. *The terrain*
4. *The leadership*
5. *Discipline*

These five constant factors should be familiar to every general. He who masters them wins; he who does not is defeated.

Ok, so that was all in military words. How does this relate to your marketing and business strat?

The way (or in some translations of Sun Tzu, the moral influence) my dear friends, is pretty much the same as speaking about your marketing resolve. Are you marketing on-purpose with sufficient conviction that you believe in your products and services, and have you mustered the energy to drive this to success? Get it: do you believe in yourself? If you do not have this conviction, I will not fight with you! I will be wasting my time. You have to believe in what you are doing to succeed. Take a look at Tony Robbins for example. He believes in his products and believes in what he does; so this belief underscores his marketing efforts and leads him to success, invariably.

The weather, Amigo, is whatever outside forces impact on your marketing efforts. *Oh, we're in a recession, so can't expect much sales Oh, CPI rates show average household income is less expendable than ever before, so hey, we're lucky to make a sale, and very grateful for the little we can get*. Can you anticipate my answer to all of that? That's right – Bullshit! Big fucking dollops of cow dung and fly infested bullshit Amigo! Your weather should only be things like being stuck on a 3G device with limited bandwidth instead of connected to some LAN cable or where Wi-Fi has 4G coverage at LTE speeds. Got it? Your weather is Coca Cola just sent a tsunami of marketing campaigns out and we're not matching them!

The terrain is quite simply your market place. It's where all the action is happening. Has your business department fed you sufficient data about your target market yet? Can you with ease tune into your demographics – the right followers, people, geo-locations, what's your product? What promo will appeal to them, what pricing are you using? Blah-blah-blah. You get it? Cyberspace is your fucking market place darlings – there's like almost four billion people online, and counting. There's no borders there. There's only time and language barriers, and even then, there's nothing Google Translate can't do! Who are your competitors, huh? Do you even know? Shit man, make your notes now!

The leadership or Commander, as some Sun Tzu translations show, is simply your leadership. Who is the brains behind your marketing, mmm, Mr. uh, CMO, right? Or is it the CIO? Don't know, don't care, how does that sound. I don't fucking care who is the hot shot, because he is not the one on the battleground making split-second decisions on your brand. Your social voice, whoever is working things online is the one! And I'm sorry for you, if that employee is not a leader. You need a good fucking seasoned, battle-hardened leader to run things there, CMO/CIO. If you've just got some sheep responding to your authority, God help your fucken company, because you are going to fucken sink in cyberspace!

Discipline or doctrine refers to the guiding principles you're using for your war strat. What principles are going to translate into your online success? Sun Tzu, right!

So, these 5 factors make up your online assessment. Do you have the will power, the resolve to do this? Do you have the means to market online and can you reach your enemy (or can they reach you for that matter)? Do you have the right leadership or rather line-of-command to give effect to your strategy, and what strategic principles are you going to employ?

Jot these down, and if you cannot meet any of these 5 factors, do something drastic until you can, because without these things, there will be no war ... you will lose before you even start.

Now, having said this much, let me remind you what I said before, strategy ends in your business. Your business is what happens behind the scenes of the battle online, and it needs to be a coherent whole. If your marketing tells you, we need more R&D, we see competitors are launching new products, new branding, new whatever the fuck ... you had better move swiftly to fill a potential vacuum. Because novelty fills vacuum online more than anything else. Fashions, trends, novelties ... all these things come and go, and you can make a shit load of money if you're positioned to fight on these fronts at the right time. Got to be vigilant, but we'll cover that later in this book.

The assessment you do here needs to carry some kind of recommendation of how the fuck you are going to increase business with your existing followers and customers. Note I said *existing*!

There is a great degree of research that has shown that people who know, especially those who have previously bought from you, are more likely to buy from you, again and again. And also note this *assessment* is not your strategic plan!

What you want to do here is to dig into those underlying causes to explore avenues as to why you are not making it per your vision right now. And what can you do to improve your marketing with this assessment?

Profile your Online Customer

Part of your strategic assessment is in identifying and profiling your customer. So, let's take a closer look now, at your customer. We need to find out why is this chap going elsewhere for your products and services? We need to see who is this chap going to and why is he going there instead of to you? What do *they* have that you don't? Who are they? *They* in this context are your competitors.

So, the first thing we want to determine is who exactly are your online customers? By getting to know who we want to target as our prized online commodity – I mean face it, these prospects are your gold, man! They're the riches, the wealth you are after. You want to refine them through your conversion processes from raw prospects and leads into hard-core customers, hungry and unsatisfied by having just *one* product off your shelves, or *one* service off your lines. Get it?

You are from now on going to pay attention to their needs and wants and how best you can fill the vacuum. You see, it doesn't matter what you have or offer – it matters what they want and need. Got it? Who is your customer anyway? Have you profiled them properly?

Here's what you do before we proceed: Jot down who your customer is, and don't give me EVERYONE! Of course it is everyone – and there's like 7-billion of everyone out there. Let's get real; narrow this profile down to something manageable, you can't easily go after EVERYONE! We're looking to launch an attack, our first attack; so we have to be certain whom we are going to nail first.

Who's your customer?

I want you to jot down male and female with a dividing line. Under each heading show age group. Who's your ideal customer? Who is most likely to engage with you, and buy your products and services? Right.

Next line, what is their station in life – are they married, single, divorced, what? Does it matter? Fuck yeah! Married couples will Q n A things longer than singles. Ok, now tell me what their earning profile is. Are they swimming in it? Or are they in need of credit? Is your product a necessity or a luxury to them? Can they afford what you are letting it go for?

Next line – what kind of jobs do these customers have?

Next line, list out their interests, hobbies maybe.

I had a client once who wanted to do some targeted advertising, but they couldn't get around this demographic concept. They had Persian carpets on sale. All they knew was you got to target 45-60-year-old females. I looked at that and told them to think out the box a bit.

Who's your customer? In this case it was someone interested in buying a luxury item. And since a Persian carpet increases in value over time, I was told, I advised my client to place golfers in the demographic. You see, who plays golf? Someone with money, right. To stereotype the golfer, it's the dude whose hair is turning grey on the tips, who drives an SLK, who networks with other Execs on the greens. A customer who can buy doesn't necessarily have to specify Persian carpets listed in their interest categories to be targeted. You got it? We ran the ad; zoomed in on the identified audience, and what happened? Let's just say my client got the highest sales to date for *that* month! And of course, I got a healthy comm as a bonus! SO, wrap your attention around this for now – who's your customer?

Next thing in our list of demographics is: what other things – like products and services – is your customer most probably interested in? If you're selling gold clubs, your customer is probably also interested in golf-shirts, caddy bags, and classy watches! Right, so our list enables us to get a clear profile of whom we are going to target. To shoot with a come-buy-me message. To poison-their-minds into wanting our products. To make-them-slaves, addicts to our stuff, so they cannot get enough, and become dependent on our offering. This is what we are after here.

Know your customer. Who is he/she/they? Is it even an individual? Is your customer maybe a collective, like a company? Same principle. Get to know who will buy from you!

We are so blessed with current technology that much of this customer profiling data can be obtained from various analytic platforms available both on social media, and on website monitoring software. Much of this software can even determine where your customers are – as in geographically. This is freaking excellent especially for recruiters and staffing professionals who target candidates living in proximity to certain business nodes, and the likes.

You may even want to develop another section of your target customer profile: call it what key brands they associate themselves with. I'm serious about this!

I once worked as a property broker, renting retail space for shopping malls. Man, that was an exciting job! I will never forget I cold called on a mid-tier fashion brand; and my counterpart within the brand told me they will only consider signing a contract if I had signed up a particular bank and a certain mobile provider as tenants. I hadn't had any of the brands suggested by this fashion client. So, I went back to the drawing board, and approached the suggested brands. After some lengthy negotiating, and hard, nerve-wrenching closing tactics, I eventually got them signed, and went back to the fashion brand. I showed the brand the signed contracts for the bank and mobile tenants, and voila, without even batting an eyelid, they signed and transferred deposits without delay.

So, what's the moral of the story here? Some brands tend to be grouped with different consumer preferences – so you want to be vigilant of these preferences, as these make good for targeting when doing advertising campaigns and the likes. And ... get this, for timing your own content.

What? That's right! You will want to monitor when those brands post things from their platforms or run their campaigns – because this is when your customer will be online!

In Sun Tzu's time, the village maidens who would collect water would wait until the rivers reached a particular flow, and would then come out to play – leaving their villages vulnerable and open for attack. Same concept here – your customer will naturally be there when they are pulled to other things they like; and if your content, your ad, your messages get fired at the same time, happy days ahead!

Now, remember in the beginning of this profiling section, I mentioned your customers are currently *buying* from your competition. Why are they not buying from you?

You want to turn all your attention now onto your competition to understand *why* them and not you. We want to define the war zone now – and the only way to do this, is to know whom we are up against.

If you know, or you think you know, who your competition currently is; then write these down as well. Now. What we want to do is to find out what makes these fuckers strong, or weak in terms of whom we are? What is so appealing about these competitors that our customers go to them?

Right, we do a SWOT analysis – sure you must have heard about this somewhere along the line in business planning? SWOT: Strengths, Weaknesses, Opportunities and Threats – the defining variables of our competition.

SWOT the Competition

Sun Tzu used the SWOT? Sure he did! In the strategic assessment we have basically revealed what your strengths are and where the opportunities lay within your internal organisation to catapult your marketing efforts to new heights.

Now, we're turning the focus slightly to the external factors of these strengths and weaknesses.

To complete your strategic assessment, you need to weigh up what is happening in cyberspace with your brand. So, here you need to be really objective and call a spade a spade. If your position is shit, state it as a fact. You can never deal with reality if you deny it.

There's two ways to do what Sun Tzu demands. One is conducting a thorough competitor's analysis. Two is to do a benchmark study. Usually you need a prior competitors' analysis from which to benchmark future evaluations, so decide which works best for you. Only, with benchmarking, avoid falling in the trap of comparing yourself with obvious giants! I mean really, if you are just Jacks' Dealership in second hand cars, don't now go and benchmark yourself against some BMW franchise up the road. You're just not in the same league yet, obviously! You will get there in due course, but for now, select competitors who are on a par with you more or less. When you get to the top of that selected league, set your sights on something bigger. I'm also not saying not to dream big, fuck yeah! Dream huge dude, I only encourage you to, just you know, do what is real, get it. Step by step we will get you to huge and beyond.

The SWOT analysis we do now will be included in your competitor's analysis in the next section. So, understand all these mini-studies, assessments, comparisons … call them what you are comfortable with, are essentially one thing leading to the next in better understanding the game-plan or the strategy we will decide on adopting once done with all of this. So, bear with us; it is a process, and your victory is all in this planning! So, let's do it right.

Of course, if you have a lot of money and would rather let experienced veterans in the game do this for you, then trust me, I have the right team who can do this for you, yet this is bar the point here: whatever it takes, get this data down. Write it down! You need to get it in front of your nose, and see the state of digital affairs for what it is!

And whilst you're doing this, a word of caution: we're planning at this stage to go to war. Make sure those in your war room are sworn to fucken secrecy! You do not wish to advertise through some stupid update to the effect that we're doing a competitive analysis of our market, or we're undertaking a strategic assessment so we can position ourselves as better than some F500! You do not want your social media person to shit in their pants and go running off to apply for a post with your competitor at this stage. Get it.

#justsaying!

And my second caution is, don't now go halt what you're doing online whilst you regroup with your planning. In fact, don't even tell your social media or marketing team a damn thing until we've worked this all out. Let them carry on with their one or two updates a day for now. Let them continue posting crap on your networks. You want to take your fucken enemies by surprise; so let them laugh, and mutter to themselves, pooah! That stupid hardware store on the corner of 4th and 10th! They're nothing. Keep them thinking like this, while you work this assessment to the bone.

#getfuckenbusy!

Check out what Sun Tzu has to say about this:

> Every general has heard of these five things. Those who know them prevail; those who do not know them do not prevail.
>
> Therefore, use these assessments for comparison, to find out what the conditions are. That is to say,
>
> 1. Which political leadership has the Way?
> 2. Which general has ability?
> 3. Who has the better climate and terrain?
> 4. Whose discipline is effective?
> 5. Whose troops are the stronger?
> 6. Whose officers and soldiers are the better trained?
> 7. Whose system of rewards and punishments is clearer?
>
> This is how you can know who will win.

Let's put this in simple English. From your assessment, you covered 5 factors: the way, or moral influence or resolve to succeed; the weather, or climate that is likely to impede any marketing efforts; the terrain, or market place; the leadership – or rather the guiding hand driving the marketing team; and lastly, the discipline

– that is to say the principles in which your strategy will be executed. You might want to have these outlined in a document of sorts.

So, based on these 5 strategic areas of assessment, Sun Tzu now advises us to address another 7 areas in terms of each of these 5 factors.

So, Q1 is quite simply to determine which competitor has the resolve to succeed in the digital market place. This is quite interesting, because a quick overview of your competitors' digital presence, usually evident by way of their websites and social media presence, will show how they are doing. If they have obvious graphically designed material, with sharp, innovative and modern designs, then you know these bastards have budget to throw at graphic designers – who are not exactly cheap!

You will also very quickly see who is doing it and who is not. Tell-tale signs are your competitors have fancy, classy looking websites with all kinds of functionalities, which we will deal with later on in this book. Or alternatively, they have a really crappy looking presence, or outdated from the 80s and 90s still. Then you know they have either paid attention to their digital marketing or simply do not have budget to commit to anything great.

Easy enough, huh? And you can test their resolve on any of the 5 factors. On the terrain they will show to what extent they are present – you will see their ads, their polls, their branding and info and all that stuff. If it's not there, they're not doing it, and you immediately have the advantage to claim the terrain as yours. Annex your space in cyberspace. Looking at their leadership – is their CMO and CEO on social media? Do they speak about their brand from their personal pages – you'll be surprised what you will find here! Many companies have a surprising low presence, but their leadership sells them, because of fame or association, or whatever. You will see when you answer this one.

Weather – by inference you will see if they are doing it or not, and why. Discipline – also pretty easy to spot: they are usually doing their social media especially in-house when you see plenty staff pics and functions; and they outsource when you see a lack of personal presence in many cases, low engagement, standard posts ... boring essentially. Not trying to shoot down marketing agencies here, just an observation in most instances of what you are likely to find. So, if you are a marketing agency reading this book – take this as some uncanny advice to pull up your socks before you lose your client.

Coming to the second question, which general has ability? This pretty much goes hand-in-glove with the previous question, and here you need to draw your own conclusions through inference of your observations. It will also show you who you are up against.

Who has the upper hand in climate and terrain – in obstacles and market place? Have a look at their following and ranking in the digital space. Which would you be more likely to engage with – a brand who has 100k followers or one with only 100? Or a brand whose posts are like clocking it man, 2-300 likes a post; or 2-3 likes if lucky? You get it? Of course, you will be attracted to the stronger one.

Turning to effective discipline – there's a clear and distinct difference between Coca Cola's marketing versus the local milk-man! It's all in the team behind the brand. We conducted an impromptu study one day by checking out a handful of household brands, and how they were doing. One in particular was an electronics brand, who took it for granted that because they were dominant in the market they needn't attend to their online customers. After all, any complaints – the customer should simply go to their nearest service store, right? Wrong! What happened?

Some boyfriend of a certain staff member at that brand, took offence to his girlfriend having cheated on him. So, this cat posts some explicit porn - tarnishing her name, *and* the brand in the process. Now, bar the legalities of deformation and all that stuff, let's cut the lovers brawl out of the equation – you see the *brand* suffered damage here, because so many people logged-on and commented, and roped the brand into the debacle, and all. My question is this – where the fuck was the brands' digital admin? I mean Facebook presence with no voice behind it? Automated posts via Hootsuite, and nobody checking in on customer complaints, reviews, suggestions, compliments ... all that kind of stuff that would make the brand social ... You get it? What a balls up!

Another instance, the brand, this time a restaurant was online; but could not handle an irate customer who complained about the food and the shocking service they got. So, the administrator of the page responded with no remorse, or reality shown by the brand, ended up drawn into a tiff, and told the customer to fuck off! Woooh! You see, discipline – you can't do that kind of stuff or allow this kind of stuff to happen to your brand online. Reputation is at stake; hell, capturing future followers, attention, and business is all at stake too.

I hope this is all sinking in, guys. You want to win at this, you have to develop every single one of these things Sun Tzu listed. Otherwise your head is going to be chopped off, your brand pillaged and plundered and absolutely buried online – and you WILL feel it offline too, in your daily in-store and day-to-day business domicile activities.

Question 5 – whose troops are stronger: aka whose following shows the best engagement? Brands with more engagement are the brands who are converting leads into real business man. Many brands have huge following counts – ten to one I bet they bought followers. Meaningless exercise in most cases, because they are of no quality. But look here, if you have a qualitative following base, you will find you have followers engaging with you. Signs of engagement are sharing, liking, commenting on your stuff. Signing up for your newsletters and subscribing to your blog updates, and all kinds of promo you throw out there. I am placing the follower under this analogy of troops here – because those who engage with you and become your brand ambassadors in some way or another. They share you to their following, their networks – and spread the word that you are alive! Get it? Of course, the troops in this instance are your marketing team too. So, you will look at the quality of your competitors in this instance to determine who is stronger and conversely who is weaker. What is the pecking order man?

The following question leads on from the troops scenario: whose officers are the better trained amongst your competitors? Dude, take a look at the leaders of your competition. I found something very funny – here in South Africa where I am currently writing. You know, there's the political party, and you got 3 dominant powers in the political landscape here: the ANC (African National Congress), the DA (Democratic Alliance), and the EFF (Economic Freedom Fighters). Looking at their political leadership here, the ANC, led currently by Jacob Zuma in comparison to Julius Malema of the EFF, and Musi Maimane of the DA have very interesting stories to tell. Did you know, the DA outsource their social media presence to subordinates within the party; whilst Jacob Zuma has only a zero-rated parody account? But - and this is interesting, Julius Malema runs his own Twitter handle! That's right, Malema tweets himself; well he did at one stage anyway! Compare his following amongst his competitors and it is quite shocking who is ahead, and far more engaged than the rest here. So, you get the idea – the leadership behind the scenes of all the daily marketing activities and PR running in cyber-space is what you must assess.

This brings us to the last question – whose system of rewards and punishments is clearer? What are your competitors doing to retain their customers and prospects? Are they giving out freebies in exchange for subscriptions? Are they giving out shout outs for good stuff originating from followers? Are they having competitions and making a big hoo-ha about the winners?

Last note on this before we move onto the competitors' analysis – in Sun Tzu's quote, he stipulates, that doing this assessment is how you will know who will win. Like I said, we will see the pecking order emerge amongst your competitors and exactly where you fit in. Keep your SWOT notes for now – these are pretty much an overview, just to orientate you in the war about to be fought.

Compile a Competitor's Analysis

Tell me something, I mean this just out of interest ... does your marketing team even *know* who your competitors are? If they do, it may be advantageous. Get them to start daily monitoring your competitors' sites and networks, until it becomes routine. It is strategic and a damn good discipline to be developed, nurtured and to be vigilant of.

I say so, because I once did a post I thought was absolutely brilliant, when I still did community management. It was a leaf with some date on it. So I posted it with words to the effect, you know what to do with this leaf today (as in turn over a new leaf) in celebration of Spring Day. Absolutely chuffed with myself, I was horrified when the client phoned up all hysterical, *Phoenix, what the fuck have you posted*? I'm like, yeah, I know, brilliance hey, sheer brilliance - you know ... full comm cycle, smiley face and all. She spat back – *then why the fuck are all our freaking competitors commenting about smoking weed*? I was like, no way, what you talking about? And then I navigated to the post, and BAM, it hit me between the eyes; I had posted a picture of a cannabis leaf! I say no more.

The point is your competitors are watching you like a hawk. They're waiting for you to fuck up, so they can pounce on your marketing efforts and drag you through the mud. Why should you not be in the same position to take them on?

I'm also not saying to get all nasty and sarcastic about it now either. You want to be the strong party in the market, not an asshole. These fuck-ups are all opportunities for your brand to counter the competition, and you need to be there to do it!

One more thing – it should never matter what your competitors are posting, really. The idea is to be aware of the trends, so you can find ways to capitalize on these, and secondly, you should in any event be so focused on your own content efforts, that you dominate online engagement with whatever you post.

Ok, here's what I want you to do:

List your competitors now, in no particular order, 1-5. If you have more, then just name them and jot them down. Look at these fuckers. They're all *your* competitors – your *enemies*! Why? Because they are attracting the same followers, and presenting themselves as options for your followers to click onto.

Now, there's unsaid rules, all placed there by democracy, so the game is, your followers have fucken *carte blanche*. They can do as they damn-well please. They can check in by you and click away to your competitor and check in there, and go elsewhere too. You understand? Your customer is your food! He's your energy, you cannot afford him to click away and cough up some cash elsewhere. You need him to spend that cash on you!

Your competitor essentially *steals* from you. Get the point? So, complete your assessment first by answering Sun Tzu – the sovereign is your competitor! Which competitor is demonstrating the greatest resolve in the war for followers?

We can use some fancy words here, like customer acquisition. Do you like that? Because that's what this is. The art of acquiring customers and ensuring these motherfuckers give us money for our stuff. Yeah!? Which commander (aka social media team, the voice behind each of your competitor brands) shows to be the most capable? Which of your competitors has better infrastructure and better-defined market audiences (aka weather and terrain)? Which competitor seems to be headed along some strategic direction (implementing decree)? Which competitor has the upper hand, the strength, the fucken clout to smack your marketing totally to the side-lines (superiority of arms)? Which competitor has the better-trained social media teams? Which competitor shows more discipline in meting out rewards and punishments (they're just somehow whacking it out on all platforms every day, with competitions and all kinds of innovations to keep their platforms lively and followers engaged)?

Get the data – that's what I am saying here. As an additional value-add, at the end of this book is a link that you can follow to get a free Competitors Analysis Template to guide your research.

In the meantime, here's what you do to compile your own digital competitors' analysis:

Step 1: Locate your competitors online

From your list of 5 or so identified competitors, add to it what their cyberspace addresses are: I want you to make a list of their website url's, all their social media handles, hell, look into their About Us sections on their websites and list out *their Generals* and kin.

I want you to be able to find these fuckers online. I want you to know where they are located, so you can study them and get to know them better than they know themselves!

Know your enemy, beginning with your competitor.

Step 2: Prepare 3 comparative grids

Hey! Stop scratching your head and take that frown off your face! I'm about to elaborate on these grids, ok. The purpose of each grid is to segment specific kinds of comparative data we're about to immerse ourselves in. First, website presence and performance. Second, social media presence and performance. Third, the kind of content we find on each platform and how the competitor is using their content to drive traffic (a nice descriptive word for tons of followers, leads, consumers, prospective customers and so on).

Once we have compiled all the data to complete these grids, we will then return to our SWOT analysis previously done, and combine our findings from the grids into that SWOT – to give a macro-view of the SWOT so to speak.

That's easy enough, right? So for now grab 3 separate pages and each will be their own grid. Your first grid we are going to label "Website Performance". The second grid, "Social Media Performance" and the third, "Content Strategy".

Just a bit about content here – sure you must have heard the adage by now, Content Is King! Yeah? All hail content! And yes, bow to it brothers and sisters, we're slaves to content. Without content – in whatever form, be it visual, auditory, text-based, or combinations of these, content is what will fuel your sales engine, your online existence. Without content, you will not be found. I repeat, without content you will not be fucking found! Get that! SEO hooks into your content, or rather your content provides SEO the keys to index you in search engines so you can be found. And in any event, it is your voice in digital media. So obviously we need to see how your competitors are using their content.

Having categorized these grids, we now need to populate them. So, before we do so, I want you to mark off a left hand margin column on each grid – which will pretty much be your reference point for the analysis of each competitor you will be tracking.

So, with Grid 1: Website Performance, your left hand column will list each of your competitors' names – i.e. brand name or company name, whichever you are analyzing; and directly under each name you are going to put their website url. Leave sufficient room for 4 equal size columns to the right.

Coming to Grid2: Social Media Performance, your left hand column will again list each of your competitor's names, only this time with their respective social media handles. Now, here you will have to be super-organized with your data. What I suggest is to have one page to group each competitor so you can compare one social media platform per page. So, you will for example list out all your competitors and their handles for Facebook on one page; then the same but their Twitter handles on another, and so on.

Grid 3: Content Strategy, your left hand column – just simply list out the competitors, no need for handles or url's here; simply because you're going to be looking at the overall content here.

You might want to do this analysis in Word (or Pages on Mac), in landscape view to make it easier, and in table format, so you can add more rows if needed. Do it in PowerPoint (or Keynote on Mac) if you want to get really fancy and make it visually appealing to some board.

I also suggest you add pages to each grid so that you can group the things you are analyzing. By this I mean, you will have one page dealing with your website analysis. Another page dealing with any other website's the Competitors' Generals may have – like their own blogs or personal websites; or even additional websites at your competitor's disposal. You may find one competitor has 3 or 4 different websites all feeding into the same strategy here.

An absolute LEGEND whose content I follow may best illustrate this point. His name is Grant Cardone; you may have heard of him? He's *the* International Sales Guru … in fact, he IS *THE* Godfather of *Sales*. He also does significant social sales. Do yourself a huge favour folks, head on over to any of his sites, or his social media, sign up for every newsletter and service you can, because man, this dude is ultra-dynamic! He will motivate the pants off of you and get you selling like never before! He has a couple of golden websites that I follow. Here's a few that I am familiar with:

    grantcardone.com
    grantcardonetv.com
    cardoneuniversity.com
    cardoneondemand.com
    secretstoclosingthesale.com
    addictedtosuccess.com
    10xseminar.com
    10xeverything.com
    100waystostaymotivated.com
    millionairebooklet.com

And the list goes on! Quite a guy this folks! You get the point I am making here though: make a separate page to compare each company's website or person's website.

The same for their social media comparatives. You will want, firstly for the identified competitor, and then secondly you want to compare each of the competitor's Top Leaders or Generals vs. each other. Don't now go and compare a brand vs. an individual – that's not a real comparison. Compare brands vs. brands and people vs. people, ok.

Step 3: Add the competitors to each grid

You are free to innovate here with whatever you feel necessary and appropriate to compare between all your competitors. However, to make things easy on you, I have selected what I think are the best comparatives to base your analysis on.

Go back to Grid 1. List the columns going right – first, Global Web Rank; second, Country Rank; third, Bounce Rate; fourth, Number of Websites Linking In. As I said, you are free to add more columns if you feel you need more comparative variables on which to base your analysis. There's plenty data out there that can even compare things like number of pages viewed, average time spent per page view, average time spent on website; average number of pages viewed per logged-in session. Blah-blah-blah. I take these for a very good reason as it cuts through all the bull-shit and walks the fine line to give you both the bigger picture of the state of affairs in the competitive environment, digitally; as well as a bit of detail from which you can draw some effective insights.

Feel free to add as many competitive variables you think will be useful to your analysis. I have given you the guidelines above; you are free to use your discretion and discernment when selecting the relevant criteria against which you will compare each competitor.

Then under Grid 1, I want you to add another page and call it digital strategy. Same competitors with url's in the left hand margin. Only this time, your columns must include the headings: Social Media Integration, Blog, Subscription Sign-Up, and Website Aesthetics.

Also add in an Observation Page for what you note your competitors are doing on their websites that are unique against what the others are doing. It's obviously working for them, that's why they're doing those things, whatever they are. It does not mean those things will necessarily work for you on your website, but it's good to know. Why? Because your followers are finding those things interesting enough to lose their loyalties for your brand!

Also add another page with the same framework, only the columns will be numbered 1-5. You can go up to any number you want though, whatever makes your toe nails curl! This page will be your SEO report, and you will browse on Google like a follower, prospective customer, to try find your competitor, and you're going to note your findings here. More about this process in a minute.

Lastly, another SEO page, same as the one you just did – but you will be using this to list the top brands/companies who actually did turn up in search results. Here's the R-Factor for you – the brands you listed might not be the competitors you need to watch in any event! You will see why further down. But just plant that seed in your skull for now, and stay vigilant as to whom your real competitors are!

Don't worry about where we are going to find the data for now – don't get ahead of yourself. We're just setting up a framework for analysis at the moment. We will shortly return to fill in the blanks.

Right, moving on to Grid 2 – fill in these columns now: Page Likes (or Follower Count if you prefer); Post Regularity; Engagement. Take your engagement column and break this into 3 sub columns – post likes, shares, comments.

Grid 3 – add these columns – Aesthetics and Type of Content. Subdivide the type of content into Pictures (or Graphics if you want to sound fancy), Articles, Videos, Quotes, and Links. And again, add whatever you feel appropriate here. I've done competitors that have included mobile apps and podcasts in the analysis too, so just add whatever would be appropriate and relevant. In other words, the competitors' analysis you conduct is fully customizable.

Step 4: Enter the data into Grid 1

Excited? I'm exposing you to another world now. If you are tired, or in need of a pee break, or some coffee, water, or food – go attend to those things first, and then come back to this section. You need to be wide-awake for this! This is the gold man. This is the good stuff!

Ready?

Hit your address bar with this url: alexa.com.

Brilliant site this. You can and should subscribe to it, as in buy its services. Alexa basically pumps out data on website performance, and for any website's you may be interested in for comparative purposes. Ok, scroll down the Alexa's landing page until you find a search box? This is where you enter your competitors' website url. And of course your own! Ok, hit the enter key and give it a few secs, and up pops a full-on report.

My suggestion is you navigate up and down to familiarize yourself with the indicators, and take special note of the data we're looking for. You will easily see the global rank of the site in question, and its rank in particular countries. Most websites will rank in the USA first before they rank anywhere else – but if your website has a suffix other than .com – like say .co.za for South Africa, and the website is doing particularly well there, then it will show the little ZA flag with its rank.

Excellent performing websites will generally rank from #250,000 in the world right up to #1. Poorly ranking websites will pretty much fall off the scale at 12-mil and over. Just shows you how many websites there are in the world. Yup – over 1-billion websites world-wide! So to rank 12-mil out of 1-bil is still pretty good.

And of course, you will fill in all the blanks on your grid. Number of sites linking in is found down towards the end of the Alexa report – and is pretty much an indicator of how many websites or linkages your site has to other sites in the world. The more the merrier folks! Shocking to find that sooo many websites hardly have any of these. These linkages generate referral traffic; so best you learn how to create these.

On Digital Strategy you want to take a look at the qualitative aspects of the website. Alexa is your quantitative data. To see if there is any social media integration, simply look for the cute little social media icons. Ideal scene is to have these on every page, where they are easily accessible. Most well-integrated sites display these icons in the header of the site, which is where I prefer them to be. In the footer, you still have to scroll down, and often if in a hurry, who the fuck scrolls down anymore, right?

However, social media icons are not enough! You need other things like social media share buttons, so you can share from the site you're on, instead of clicking on it and being routed to the brands' social media pages. There should be login's too when you do so. Check for any social proof widgets – like sidebars especially for Twitter and Facebook. Also check if the website shows any social pictures or video's linking for instance to Instagram and YouTube. You get the picture? Also – and this one is laughable yet pretty serious: click on each icon and see where you land up. I have often found, especially on F500 sites, the icon clicks to a 401 or 405 page! Not found! Pity. Or some are simply there for show, they don't even click through anywhere! You might also want to click on the share buttons, to see if they work.

You see, the data you get from this exercise will very quickly show you where your competitors weaknesses are. And will also highlight what the fuck you need to be doing on your own website. You want to be found, and you want your customers to land on you without losing them. Somehow your website has to be like a spider web to trap them and keep them, so you can gobble them up for all they are worth!

Just keeping it real, folks. Of course I don't mean it literally like that. But you want their business!

Check for signs of a blog. You will be shocked at how many sites don't have a blog. I mean that is like committing digital suicide. Blogs are gold! You quote them in your content mix on social media, they also get indexed in Google, so always somewhere, someone is finding your website more than likely from a blog posted on social media, and they can read the full version on your site; and once in your site, you can hook them, and convert them into a sale, and make money!

Also check for a newsletter or some kind of subscription sign-up. Your website needs to be able to keep track of its visitors. Something that gets their email address, at least! Or even their mobile number. Do you know how effective email and sms campaigns are? Yeah, they stem from this one little thing on your website: somebody is given the option to sign up for a free giveaway, like an eBook, or a report, or a newsletter, or some free consultation, or service, or whatever the fuck it takes to get their email. They opt-in – make it easy for them boys – and you get their contacts, and then you have an asset in your system. You are one step closer to being able to close them sooner or later on your products and services.

Then, the general aesthetics of the site – give it a rating on a scale of 1-10, or a % if you please. Bottom line, does their website look shitty? So, shitty that you will bounce right off and run for the next competitor? Or does it look like OMG, out of this world – I just got to have a look inside and get something, and come back for more, and OMG tell my friends about it! You get the picture here?

Fun hey? Yeah, that's what I'm talking about! Let's get this Grid 1 section to a done.

I already briefed you on the observations of your competitor's websites here. So, list them out competitor by competitor; listing out the unique features you see. Whatever these may be. The site has a slider that rotates compelling images; or a little pop up thingy sees you and texts you how it can help; or you see specials on products; or win this and that; or whatever. Write these observations down. Very important. We want at the end of this analysis to be able to get your brand offering something different, or doing something different than the rest. Make yourself extraordinary, not average. Alternatively, we may want to learn from our competitor's successes and possibly incorporate similar elements into our own forward strategy.

SEO – head on over to Google. The first is taken from Alexa – where it shows the top 5 keywords people Google to find the particular site in question. You might see patterns here across the different competitors, where common keywords are identified that will get them found. Once done, take off the analyst hat, leave Alex, and think like a layman. If you find that a challenge because of personal bias or whatever, get one of your kids or a friend to do this exercise. Type in 5 separate industry words you would type if you were looking for services and products in your industry. So, like if your product is shoes, you will type in shoes, shoe stores, leather shoes, high-heels, sandals and so forth. Don't type these in all at once … I mean type in for 5 different searches. You know what I mean! Take special note of the brand names that pop up in search results. And list these out in order they appear. You may be surprised to find your competitors show up only in some searches and not in others; they may not even show up at all. But others do, who you were unaware of that these are your competitors.

Use your own discretion here now. Obviously a dominant brand in the market who is a million times your size, is no competition for you, yet. They will chew you up and spit you out quicker than you dial 911. So, you do not want to list them as a competitor. List those who you can see can match you or who are slightly better than you – as a competitor that is. The idea is you want to have some competitors to beat on the way up, whilst you strive to gain ground on the most dominant competitors in your industry.

Having done so, you may want to relook your competitors for the rest of this analysis; and maybe adjust who you are going to analyze. In which case you will need to start over – or hey, why not simply add them to the ones you already identified as competitors? It matters not, because it will only help to clarify your forward position, your forward strategy to rise to greatness. So, please, I urge you to spend some time on this part; a lot can come out of it to benefit you.

Having worked on several recruitment brands, I was able to determine the various service offerings listed on each competitor's websites. In this way the client was advised to undertake several operational actions, such as consolidate certain services under new trendy service titles; and in other instances to offer other services where they could definitely gain an edge on their competitors.

Step 5: Enter the data into Grid 2

Social media is where it's happening folks. If you're not on social media, you're not ON. You're off, and relegated to the electron dump in cyber space and your future existence in business.

For this section, there's two ways to do this. One is a laborious method, the manual physical counting method. The second is to use software – you have to subscribe and pay for this software. If you're serious about getting your brand to where you see it – then buy into this. There's several software platforms to access here: socialbakers.com and sproutsocial.com for outstanding analytic services. Course, there's a horde of these out there, and you are free to use the one's you are happy with. There's also a brilliant service offered by rivalfox.com for this purpose. Check these out and select whichever suites you best.

Personally I would sample the last 3 months of data available, but you can do it over a year if you like. Quarterly data is effective for immediate planning and execution of strategy, and helps you to seize the initiative and to take your competitors by surprise based on current performance.

The following count (or page likes) is easily found on the competitors' social media pages as a global figure. Enter it. Then scan through to see the frequency of their updates on each platform. Is it regular, daily, weekly, monthly? Is it irregular, as in 1 update today, 1 update 3 days back, 10 updates on the 4th, 3 updates on the 2nd and so on. Write a short description of these frequencies. Ideally active brands are on daily, with the exception of YouTube – although this is now increasingly compensated for through Periscope and Meerkat (now Houseparty). And BTW folks, you really need to be on Periscope if you are not. It is like instant social sales!

For the engagement, just simply tally the scores manually or via software over your sample of 3-months for post likes, shares and number of comments. These are called different things on different platforms – hearts, Favs, reactions, etc. You get the idea.

Just one word of caution here when it comes to interpreting these figures – one competitor may have 1,000 post likes and 20 post shares and 2 comments. Another may have 50 likes, 45 shares and 100 comments. These are not necessarily indicators that rank against each other, because we also need to account for the proportion of such engagement with the following base of the brand to see who is better than the next. Just bear that in mind.

Step 6: Enter the data into Grid 3

As with the website aesthetics, give a general opinion of the quality of the social media page here. If the images are generally pixelated and blurred, or distorted; they're not scaled properly to the social media page's prescribed dimension … then face it, that page looks like a dog's breakfast. You can also see there's a huge difference between a PowerPoint graphic and a PSE. And a remarkable difference for that of a graphically designed one! That sharp, crisp, sleek look and feel, like it crawled out of a magazine.

So, rate it accordingly. You see, it's a very good determinant on the depth of involvement a brand has with its digital market. And Sun Tzu gives us the insight into the competitor's budget here – you can by inference see, ooh this competitor is outsourcing to some pro; they got resource to throw at their marketing; or they're doing it on the cheap maybe with some in-house apprentice who has no training. That competitor, my friend, exhibits a weakness right there that you can take them to the cleaners on! Capture their market share both online and off! How's that!

In each of the headings in Grid 3, just scribble your observations on what you see. Under pictures in updates – what are they? Staff, functions, parties, industry-related, products and services, promo-types, whatever. Try to stick to any patterns you see here. Articles, if any are shared on social media, what are they about in broad terms: industry-related; thought-leadership; complimentary industries; promo, blogs (very good if they have these). You get the idea.

Videos – are they sharing interviews, product demonstrations, video-type ads, funnies, news … what? Quotes – ideal scene: not too many, unless you're in the motivational speaking or inspirational, maybe spiritual space. Quotes do not usually pull much engagement in the line of comments, which is really what you want. But they do pull shares, and many likes – you know, it's all about the networking aspect, and an easy way to have your avatar appear in someone's newsfeed that so n so liked blah. Are there any memes? People love that sort of shit. Gets them talking. Any talk is great, because it's the salesman's duty to get the talk started, so we can intelligently move the prospect onto a sale. And build relationships if not a sale. Get it.

Lastly, the links used. What is the condition of these links? Are they long and ugly looking strings of characters; or has the competitor gone and shortened them to make it more aesthetic? And what type of links can be seen? Do these links direct traffic to the website? Or away from the brand? Stupid mistake if it is the latter! That's not to say, sometimes you will need to share somebody's content, a friend, a staff member, an associate, or supplier, or whatever. Even a competitor if it justifies the end.

Step 7: Examine their content marketing strategies

Now we get to some nitty gritty's. This is as good as conducting intel ops on the enemy to determine what kinds of weapons they are using, what their ammo is like, what machinery they are using, and what the capacity is of all these things. So, get your notes in front of you again. Make another grid for all of your Competitors' Content Marketing Strategies. BTW – it's also a damn good exercise, in fact it is advisable, to whilst extrapolating all this data – both above and here – to check up on how you are doing as well. This way, you will also be able to spot your own weaknesses, vulnerabilities, strengths and opportunities in your own digital strategy.

Make a left column for each of your competitors, and then to the right you are going to make notes on the following: Calls to Action; Notable content tactics; typical hashtags used; degree of originality; cross-channel content; degree of automation; extent or scope of branding. Let's unpack the rationale behind comparing each of these facets.

Calls to Action aka CTA's, are the verbs of your content. These are the trumpet sounds for battle; the drum sound, the alarm, the battle cry for "attack!" "FIRE!" All right, cut out all the lol'ing now. Let's get serious. CTA's are just this. You tell the prospect what to do – like this, share this, contact us, watch this, check this out, click here, read further, and buy now; you get the picture. There are hundreds of CTA's content marketers use. You want to see what phrases your competitors are catching their prospects with. So, just make lists of the most common ones.

Now here's a thing – if you find a brand that has low engagement, one of the main reasons is their CTA's are not working for them. Either they've been pounded with too many of the same

CTA, so they've like become immune to them; or the wrong CTA's are being used and need to be changed to match the appropriateness of things. Just, you know, check it out!

Hashtags are those one-word joined-together without any punctuation keywords whose prefix is #. Lol – they should put this definition in the social media dictionary, right? Why a hashtag analysis? Well, these little things are somehow linked to search engines – either on the particular social media network's platform, or to Google. So, instead of people searching a word or phrase, they increasingly search a #hashtag for results, and immediately find you in search results. Brilliant feature for modern marketing, absolutely brilliant! As an example, on Twitter, I can type the hashtag #turtles into the search bar, and I will find myself on a page where anything ever mentioned on Twitter with that #turtle – whether in a video, a photo, a tweet, a handle ... I will find it here. News, whatever. See the power? And its how prospects find you online.

So, how are they finding your competitors? It's quite simple – your competitors are feeding them – Internet food. It's the worm on the end of the fishing hook, and you're the fish. It's the bait. It's the bait they are most likely to go for. If you're a car salesman, what kind of bait will you put out there? Probably stuff like #BMWsales #Mercedes #BuyABenz ... understand?

You will also find there are common hashtags your industry uses, that you should be using too. So, be thorough here – go through 3 months of content on each platform at least, on each competitor. You will more than likely find, many competitors never even use a hashtag – it could be arrogance, ignorance, or they could be using it in extravagance. Pay attention to the latter – overuse can kill your marketing efforts too.

Ok, types of tactics competitors are using in their content marketing. Have a look at their content mix; do they apply an 80/20 principle – that is to say 80% info 20% promo and sales? Or are they overkilling it? Social media especially is just this – social! People engage in social because they don't want to be sold. That's pretty arrogant, but is the state of affairs right now. It's your job to build relationships with customers over some time, and hook them into your network where they can be channeled to a sale. You want ultimately to be converting leads into business, into sales. So, this is something that has to be consistently worked at.

What kinds of content are they churning out, and is it in keeping with what you would expect to find on the particular platform? So, did they share office party pics on LinkedIn instead of sharing their views as thought leaders in their segment of the industry? Is their content appropriate to the platforms they use? Are you finding useful, industry-related content on their pages? Are they running specials and promotions? Competitions? Give-aways, are they doing publicity campaigns? Would you be attracted to click further with them based on their content? Look for the *"how"* here – how are they marketing themselves – not the *what* are they saying kind of stuff. Do they have podcasts – what are the weapons they are using to fire their messages at the market?

Even if you think it something stupid, write it down here. At the end of the day, everything will add up and make sense. You will see. Coming to the degree of originality of content; I guess there is only so much an industry can talk about, only so much info it can give out. That's where the challenge comes in for a marketer to think out the box. We're talking about ice cream … yeah, so what? Hollow cone with a dollop of melting flavored cream ontop! Ok. And that's all? That won't sell it. You have to portray it as something they want, and need.

Maslow's Hierarchy of Needs springs to mind here. Before we wax all academic now, just know this – it's not rocket science. Convince me to sell ice-cream to you … man, you need to get pictures in your mind's eye of a sexy chick on the beach licking – zoom in – close-up – the tongue drifting seductively over the creamy layer – zoom out – body shot … nice tits! Ooh, nice smile too. Oh yeah baby, that's what I'm talking about – I want a fucking ice cream now. Get it? Or how about this one: kids party … big cake with sparklers comes everyone is singing, laughing … but there's some kid in the background unwrapping a Cornetto, and the scene comes to a halt. Was that a sound? Is it a smell? Dunno … but now all eyes are turned on … the Cornetto. BAM! >>> they're like flying over to grab the box next to him, and dish out Cornettos to everyone and some slap stick title pops up about "Everyone's gift to themselves". Got it?

Just illustrating a point here folks, your competitors' content is either clichéd, stereotyped, shared, unoriginal, innovative or pure fucking genius. And to match them and be better, you need to study how they're running their content on a *daily* basis. Yes, daily! Because your survival needs to be a daily affair. Don't ever rest on your laurels and squander what you built. Always make more be productive, be industrious, *make* things happen. Do so until you breathe your last and drop your body. Rant over!

As far as analyzing data for cross-channel and automated content, firstly you need to see how consistent their content is across all platforms where they are present. Are the messages the same? Or are they simply copying, duplicating their updates on all platforms. It's not good if they are because that's firstly unoriginal and lazy to say the least. Also content needs to match the platform it is on. So Facebook needs to be social, Twitter needs to be newsy or short and sharp witty stuff, with a link to a blog maybe; LinkedIn needs to be thought leadership content, career oriented; Instagram – pics with plenty hashtags; YouTube – you know video marketing, ads, promo, all that kind of stuff. And especially when it comes to marketing campaigns – is the same thing advertised across all networks the competitor is on?

Automated content will hit you in the face as regular, robotic, impersonal type of content. I see this many times on huge fashion magazine brands. They repeat or recycle the same content 2-3 times in a day; same graphic, maybe the wording has changed slightly in each; but the point is it is all automated, pre-programed, scheduled to technically hit the sweet-spot times. Try engaging with the brand – you'll be lucky if you ever get feedback or instantaneous, or near-immediate response from them. They couldn't care less: they're about share my stuff, like it, but shut the fuck up.

That's at least how it seems. What is needed here is the personal touch, the voice behind the brand. Even if content is automated, which I also strongly recommend, otherwise you'll sink because you can't be in two places at the same time, and you can't be up the whole day. You're still human, so you have to #worksmart #workhard, right. You want to see the customer-service element come out here and learn from it, how the competitors respond. What is their response rate like? Are they on the ball, or a case of reach-neglect? Get it – they neglect those reaching for them, but take their likes and shares anyway. It's a bit unethical that.

How human is their online voice? You're looking mainly at their social media content marketing framework here – but also do check up on their website again. Their content marketing needs to speak with one voice. Learn from them.

This leads onto the last point here – what level of branding is your competitor using? Use your eyes – look for brand consistency: do their logos and straplines stand out? Do you find yourself resonating with the energy their branding projects at you? Is there any branding? Does their colour schemes do it for you? Is their branding consistent? Other terms for this may be things like corporate identity or CI.

Your branding is what distinguishes you. It's your identity and what you become known for, and it's really remarkable how many people associate themselves with a brand just because it's got a cool name or a catchy logo. This is your flag, what you stake into your market share as annexed and owned! Who out of your competitors is making their mark and owning their space? The one doing so is the one doing it, and coining it.

Step 8: Compile your brands' SWOT

You now need to do your own SWOT. In the beginning you did a SWOT on each competitor, and the above analysis has brought many more things to the fore. So, now you simply need to pull all the strings together and see how this impacts on your own brand out there. I know you are going to kick me now, because I am now going to give you the questions you should have asked of yourself when doing the SWOT for the competitors.

There is method in my madness as to why I never gave these questions up front. Firstly, you as the General and Strategist of your brand need to grapple with the complexities of observation. You need to develop your intuition and apply it to the battlegrounds we have defined. And I am sure your brand has stretched to accommodate all kinds of unforeseen variables in the equation.

To determine your own strengths, ask yourself, what characteristics of your digital existence give you an advantage over your competitors? Wrestle with this question a bit. In what way do you shine online? Be honest. Spell out 2-3 areas in which you feel you are exceptional. Spell out 2-3 things where you show initiative online. These things can range from simple statements like, *We have a strong following on social media*, to, *We are a well-known brand*. Initiatives may include things like; *We are the only agency posting the latest jobs in this niche*, to *None of our competitors post their podcasts on social media*.

Reflect on your Competitor's SWOT to find what you can be doing to be better than them, or to take the initiative where they show weakness.

To realize your weaknesses, answer: What in your current digital presence (and this also includes your current marketing efforts by the way) puts your brand at a disadvantage in comparison to your competitors? Give me 2-3 things that stand out. It may be something like, *Our content does not direct traffic to our website*. It is shared from other people's blogs and so traffic goes to them. Be honest, because all these little things will show you what to do to get you back in shape, and winning again. Identify 2-3 things that you are not doing, that you now realize you should be doing in your content marketing and digital strategy. Try to match up to those successful competitors – what are they doing? And another

2-3 points about what you may be failing to achieve when it comes to meeting the minimum standards in your industry online.

You're not posting frequently enough on social media? Well, you now know what to do. You're not promoting your brand often enough? You are failing to show your value propositions to the world. Whatever you identify in answering these things – write them down in this section.

Opportunities – reconsider each of your competitors to see where their weaknesses are, and if any of those can be exploited as opportunities by your brand. Everyone has weaknesses! Give me 2-3 things you can improve on in what you're doing online as derived from lessons you are learning of your competitors. At the same time, state in 2-3 bullet points what you are currently not taking advantage of in your online network capabilities. Maybe you are already on all social media platforms, but you're not doing what is needed?

It could be something like *the competitors are not running any competitions.* Here's an opportunity to do something and blitz the market – and their followers with your presence.

When analyzing your threats, find out what are the most likely competitive impediments or encroachments to the quality, reputation, and overall value of your cross-network social presence? You may have insufficient content flowing off your platforms? You may have realized your target audience watch more video's than read? In this case you had better rapidly develop short, sharp and impactful videos for upload. And very damn quickly jump your ass onto platforms like Periscope and Houseparty; don't rely solely on YouTube! List the areas where your brand is at risk. It may even be something like too many people have access to your social media platforms so your brand is at risk. Change the password, and let only certain individuals post things. Or you may be at risk by simply not being on a social media platform you find competitors on. You may see another competitor aggressively promoting themselves, and this may, very definitely will, place your brand at risk! Get it.

Given your SWOT findings, what would you now recommend to gain the upper hand in the market place, in relation to your target audience, and where can you, should you, be concentrating resources in the short-term?

I will leave these findings up to you. You're intelligent; I know you can answer these things.

How do you feel now? I'm sure you are now finding a greater appreciation for your brand and the agenda you should be drafting to the board to beef things up and launch your rockets.

Step 9: Determine your market share

There's some complex math's to this one, folks. I have developed a secret formula to determine what your percentage of market share is. It's based on many factors, so I'm not going to go into it here. Suffice it for now to understand that the size of your market is fairly proportional in digital terms to the amount of traffic you generate to your website, and the amount of following you reach on social media. In addition – it is the proportion of influence you hold amongst your competitors towards the followers. And what is more, is there is untapped potential you have as yet not accessed. There are other competitors in the same space you probably have not even identified as yet.

A simple way to calculate your particular share is to pie chart the follower count of each of your competitors' vs your own. The shortfall in this method is it only shows your market share against your competitors and not the industry at large. Secondly, there are also instances where several followers follow several brands, so the market share does not necessarily comprise a unique market share. Thirdly, market share would need to be defined in terms of global, regional or local market share. A .com presence may have its company based in Ireland, for instance, yet its competitor is in India; and herein we would need to define market share along different lines than geo-strategic considerations. You get the point.

To combat these shortfalls, certain factors would need to be calculated to provide for this state of affairs. Also, the market share is purely demonstrative of digital market share – and not necessarily business market share, in which case the analyst would require access to each competitors financials, and other types of data.

What I have developed to round off this analysis is a benchmarking methodology based on market share. It is in my mind a real indicator because the object of war is to capture market share, and grow your market share to become the dominant player, the dominant power in the market offline. To own your space, own your industry, to be the superpower in your market sector.

In other words, you need to have some gauge that will determine whether or not you are indeed capturing market dominance and at what rate. This will be your motivating factor that will appeal to the business-minded ROI board director when it comes to allocating the necessary budget to pursue your strategic course of action. You will be able to motivate the captivation of a further say 15-20% market share over the next quarter or year, depending on how you wish to pursue things hereafter.

That's the good news.

The bad news (for you) is, you will have to pay me to give you your market share figures. I have a much more refined system for conducting the above competitors' analysis, and have found a way to reduce the qualitative aspects into figures. These figures all go into the formula I developed, and lead to your market share % as an outcome. My formula will even tell you how much traffic you actually have access to without you even realizing it.

You can get by on all the competitors analysis data without this, but this *one* part will now really close the deal for you. So, it's up to you. I will leave the link in the back of this book to get in touch with me for this, and that is all I am saying for now, on this score.

Okay, all this said, now do your competitors' analysis and then let's turn our attention to how we're going to wage war! Before we implement any plan, we need to define the rules of engagement.

So, in other words, what policy are we going to apply to our marketing efforts?

I believe much marketing falls on its nose because many companies have done their assessments and competitors, but *few* have a *Marketing Policy* to steer them. I mean, this is a vital component to your strategy, as it is what will govern your operational domain within your marketing efforts. It is the development of the what-if scenarios, so that everyone in your team is clear and on the same page.

Dominate and Influence Systematically

Before we proceed with policy, I wish to take a brief detour to elucidate a possible alternative outcome. Until now we have premised much of this discussion on competition against our competitors. We're taking it as a foregone conclusion that our competitors are our enemies and seek to rid us from their market so they can have the lions share. We're also studying them, to dominate the market before they do so before us. Also if they are already dominating the market, we want to see how we can seize such dominance for ourselves.

There's nothing wrong with thinking this way. Life is a game of wits and survival after all, and only the strongest will win.

But …

Sun Tzu's central most approach to war is to win it without having to lift any arms! You as the primary strategist have won the war the minute the prize of war falls to your possession without having to fight anyone for it. This comes out of respect and influence. The corollary of which is fear – so your enemy gives in without a fight. Only in this context that fear is premised on respect and submission to the influence of your brand.

But what if you are a weaker brand, with practically zilch influence? Art of war is found in alliances. Building alliances. Isn't that what social media is all about folks?

It's about I like your stuff, you like my stuff; I know about you, you know about me; I'm involved somehow, connected, linked somehow to people you also need to be networked with, as you are with those I wish to be; and we both have what they're looking for. Isn't there something we can do together to both win customers, and business?

Alliances.

Get it.

In this regard Sun Tzu mentions two key things. The first:

> If you do not know the plans of your competitors, you cannot make informed alliances.
>
> Unless you know the mountains and forests, the defiles and impasses, and the lay of the marshes and swamps, you cannot manoeuvre with an armed force. Unless you use local guides, you cannot get the advantages of the land.

In other words, if you have not done your competitors analysis, you won't know the true strengths of your competitors, to decide on whether to form alliances or not. Remember, you have at least 5 competitors you have identified. You may go all the way up to 10, 15, 20 depending on how active your industry and niche is. You want to narrow the market into an "us and them" somehow. Then you can fight an enemy, divide the spoils and then subdivide for further conquest.

Another form of alliance is simply alignment. You could be aligned to thought leaders in your industry. Just because you mine gold, doesn't mean each and every single piece of content you disseminate should be about gold. There are many alignments within the industry ranging from labour to finance, to health and beauty, to just about anything else. So the idea is to make your content relevant within the context of gold, in this instance; and to align your brand with the kinds of brands that make your products and services relevant.

On the other hand, you may not need alliances. You can set your own level of market dominance simply by being out there all the time. By this I mean you have to be in the habit of making yourself known as far and wide as possible. It's a case of when someone opens their feed, they need to see you, even if they don't respond. It's a case of making yourself prevalent in the minds of your target audience.

Your armed force is your marketing and sales team. Your local guides are the analytics and findings of your competitors' analysis. Your terrain is the different platforms on which your digital marketing runs. So, if you don't know the ins and outs of Facebook, Twitter, LinkedIn and so on; if you don't know the way of Periscope, Tumblr and Snapchat, and above this know how to use your analytics to inform and guide your actions, then don't expect to find yourself in any kind of competitive advantage!

Coming to the second thing Sun Tzu addresses about the formation of alliances, is the concept of competing for alliances.

> *When the military of an effective rulership attacks a large country, the people cannot unite. When its power overwhelms opponents, alliances cannot come together.*
>
> *Therefore, if you do not compete for alliances anywhere, do not foster authority anywhere, but just extend your personal influence, threatening opponents, this makes town and country vulnerable.*

Now that's well summed up. To illustrate: in the early days of social media, I was advised not to allow competitors onto our platforms. Not to like them or interact with them; not to even share their stuff. Little did we understand back then that in so doing we were in fact defeating the purposes of social media – one of the main purposes being to expand networks and influence into a global world through cyberspace. Nowadays you need to actually participate in the market *with* your competitors.

Now, listen folks, use your discretion in what you share of your competitors if you decide on this course of action. I mean don't go now giving them free advertising of their products on your page for the sake of sharing. That's definitely not an alliance. Share thought leadership, share opinions about various topics. Share experiences about things happening within your industry. And like and comment on those things. Here's where you will form alliances.

Nothing has changed in the market dynamics from the classic stall-to-stall flea-market concept; to retail spaces, and trade fairs. I felt quite intrigued when 5 years ago I travelled through a black township in South Africa, and observed many such stalls along the side of the road, most engaged in the sales of fresh produce. In the middle of one block along the main road was a sign "Barber Shop". A block further up I noticed a sign, "Better Barber Shop"; and was elated to find on the third block a sign, "Best Barber Shop"! Talk about market dynamics, lol. Upon questioning an influential local in the area, I was fascinated to learn how on each of those blocks, the suburbs behind them each had different affordabilities, and so, the barber shop being owned by the same person had arisen through a unique set of alliances over time, giving rise to the concept now in operation.

You may have identified your strongest competitor online, and find that several do not even compare, unless combined. Here, you may wish to approach the Generals of those smaller competitors and discuss the business dynamics of your industry to see how best you could jointly capture market share through a coordinated effort of marketing campaigns, and other innovations. Here is where your strategic business will conspire *offline*.

Simultaneously, you nevertheless forge ahead at capturing followers and networks. You could agree to cooperate on CSI activities, or across educational and training bases, or even in public seminars and workshops. Whatever you can do to find common things to do, so as to gain strength against the main competitor in your pool. Over time, chipping away at that competitor's base, eroding its ability to manoeuvre in business, yours will then grow.

You may wish to adopt a totally different approach to the alliance-based strategy as well. Instead of forming alliances with competitors; you may seek out alliances with the brands that supply your competitors, and accentuate these alliances online. Getting them to sponsor talks and competitions may be some of the things you could do. Having them visible on your own social media platforms by way of shared posts, shared information, shared opinions, and so on. These are very tactical approaches within the strategy to use your alliances to your advantage.

Much out-the-box thinking needs to be done on this score. I'm not delving into all the intricacies of alliance as a strategy here. Just merely pointing out the decision you need to be aware of in the battle for market share.

Whether you dominate through alliance or through personal effort, you need to dominate your space. This will translate into dominating the market, making your brand *the* go-to/come-to brand in the minds of the customers. The best form of domination is without a doubt the self-made, self-driven personal effort at branding your space. It shows strength in purpose and also gives you a certain independence in the market place that will set you apart and unique in your offering.

Use your established dominance to influence the outcomes. In other words, when your brand is seen as the market leader; when it releases a new product/service, its reputation will precede it, and influence your followers to want more of what you got. As an example, Lady Gaga, Rihanna and Justin Bieber can pretty much say whatever they like online, do as they please, and each time they do whatever, their massive networks will respond, through engagement, sharing to their own respective networks, and purchasing all the latest hits. That is incredible influence because these celebrities dominate their online spaces with millions of fans. Compare this to a small rock group struggling to get a weekly gig at the local pub and you will very quickly see why they need to get into a position of market dominance and influence.

You need in other words to horde and amass attention in the market space. You need to treat your brand as a celebrity essentially. In a certain sense your brand leaders and brand holds some celebrity status already. Think about it, you're on social media making yourself visible to so many people, and growing each day. In yesteryear if you were seen in the media, you pretty much became famous. Social media is a form of mass media; plus, it is global. That is incredible.

Think of it like this: a force to be reckoned with in the battle field is a force that is known to hold superior power. That's exactly what celebrity status does to an individual or brand. Its fame makes its mark, and this is also the pursuit of dominance as a strategy in the field. Armies show their strengths in the form of parades, where they showcase the best of their military technologies. It is no different in the field of marketing. You need to consistently show your market your strengths, your wins, your thoughts, ideas, practical applications and benefits of your offerings.

PART 2

DOING BATTLE

Develop your Policy

The best strategy is that which obviously works best. You cannot afford to find the right strategy by excessive trial and error. Imagine all the money down the drain in that exercise? That much said, let me also state this, and I realize it sounds a bit contradictory to what I said above, to keep your strategic planning process *secret* from your team until fully developed. I am now going to say that strategy and execution should ideally work in unison. Don't waste time.

So, first thing we're going to do is to see that we have you *able* to deliver on all fronts. Remember, just because your competitor is not on Twitter, does not mean you should not be there *either*. In fact, you should ideally be on as many social media platforms as possible. The internet is capable of you being able to deliver on a unique phenomenon: the state of omnipresence. You can be pretty much everywhere you need to be all at the same time. Your followers have their own preferences which social media platforms they access; so the idea is to be able to reach them wherever they are, whenever.

Step 1 is to put you on the field so you can deliver to wherever they are. Set up your base in *their* zone. Got it? That's what I mean by running strategy and execution simultaneously for now.

The real *fuck-them we're pulling them in* for business strategy continues to be developed in the background, ok. Handle contingencies as they arise, things like black PR (we'll hammer this out in a moment), and so on.

So, back to the rules of engagement ...

The following four policies are key per Sun Tzu.

Policy #1: Invest resource to sustain your efforts

You need to relook your marketing budget, and throw as much resource at it as possible. And hey, cut that crap out that you feel your marketing is like putting your money in a bucket with holes in. Yes, marketing is a costly exercise so brace yourself for it. You cannot expect to invest $100 and get $1,000 back *right now*. In any event, back in the day when we paid for ads in print-media these worked out far costlier than what you would be spending on social media today.

Those troops in the frontline may not see any *enemy (aka. The analogous online prospect – your customer)*, but they know they're there, and fire volley upon volley to let them know, they're onto them and coming. Keep dreaming that way though, because when you do this right, you will see the scales tip and you'll make your money back, quickly too. But for now, remember they don't even know you man! Your followers don't know you. So, you got to have something to show them that you are there, and you got to let them know that. And never ever assume they know you!

You need to make marketing regular, routine, a normal basis of day-to-day operations. Never slack off. Always be out there, making yourself known. Always be attracting new business. Repeat business is a different concept. Always be pushing for new business, new customers. Repeats are a bonus. You want the new ones.

New one's don't even know who you are or what you've got for them? And right now they're sitting in your competitors' networks, smiling with them, liking their cute little pussy pictures and stupid quotes, and fails and shit. You need to show them big daddy's on the block, kids. Understand? They'll come. They'll browse and like and smile with you too. And that's okay, you want to make it comfortable for them to stay, and come back and repeat these actions. You want to lure them in for now, and build their trust – let them click away for now, so they feel they still have that power. The power to click is their safety net. Leave it in tact for now. Break that at this point in time, and fuck, you will have committed digital murder, asshole! So, be disciplined and respond to their reaches. Soft sell, got it?

Money, budgets ... don't run out of it. You want to make money, but *some* money needs to be spent on building influence and reach first. Look at it differently for now, it's not ROI spend to reap buyers yet. It's ROI to reap influence. We're manning up our battleships with social media and building our networks of influence.

Your budget is your supply line. Cut that and you are dead. So, again, to keep it real, there's the budget constraint, which will determine what you can actually do with your budget. If its small and minute, well, fuck, ok, we'll just have to engage in tinier battles than the grand boom onto the landscape in capturing market share and dominance. And anyway, your competitors all have the same argument about budget spend.

So, work it out: what is feasible for you, what is real? Note to C-Suite – don't take this as an argument to squander resources in the name of winning. I mean it needs to make financial sense too, obviously. All I am saying is allocate a *WORTHWHILE BUDGET*.

Let's say you only currently have a website, some outdated 2010 Word Press piece-of-shit theme with practically zip functionality. Let's say you're only on Facebook and Twitter. Now after the competitors, we find you need to upgrade your website as in yesteryear! Plus, you need to extend your social media influence through to LinkedIn, YouTube, Google+, Instagram, Pinterest, Houseparty, Periscope, and Vine. Plus, you need to up your blogging game seriously, do some email marketing ads, boost posts on

Facebook, sponsor posts on LinkedIn and advertise on Twitter. Remember this is just to establish yourself to be able to launch your weapons embodied in your content, online service, and marketing tactics. Oh, and you need that shopping cart plugged into your website so they can order online, and this all needs to be accessible from your social media platforms.

You could of course go the organic route. It requires zero budget. Takes forever and a day to grow anything organically online though. You know; rely on the algorithms of the various social media. Really, in this instance only your immediate network will be accessible; and let's face it, not everyone sees you online just because you posted something. If you have 2,000 friends on Facebook for example, because of the algorithm, you probably really see only 10% of your network in your feed. That's just not good enough for two reasons: one – you need more like 100,000 friends; and two – you need more than 10% seeing your posts.

Pretty much the only way to do so, to ensure this, is to throw some budget at getting your posts visible before a relevant audience; and this is where the profile of your online customer becomes useful. You can target for as little as $1 the right person to see your posts.

All it takes is that one person to just cognite on your post and decide that is what they want; the next thing you get a message, you follow up, more comm to and fro, and before you know it you land a deal, a sale … you get the point.

So … we're talking like from $1,500 upwards. That's just to establish yourself man. To run this, we're looking at anything from $500 per month upwards. Right. So, it's not that much if you think about it, compared to say what you would normally be spending on radio, newspaper (I mean WTF reads that anymore), magazine, or TV, okay. Anyway, if you're an F500, this is absolute piss for you!

It's the small guy though, man I feel for you. Maybe set the infrastructure up for yourself by yourself. That way, its far cheaper, and maybe you just need a helping hand with your website, right.

But ... you're still going to need budget for advertising and putting yourself out there.

I think you get the point though: loud and clear, allocate a feasible budget to marketing!

Policy #2: Do things timeously ... as in speedily

Budgets in place, awesome. Thumbs up, man, now we're talking. What you need now is wisdom, economy and thrift. Get it. Don't let Sun Tzu find you have wasted budget on shit! You got a marketing team, ensure these fuckers represent your brand, your company, with their fucking lives! If they do not, FIRE the fuckers!

You want your team to give stellar customer service. Why? Those followers will come to you at any time of the day or night, from anywhere on this planet. That's why. Your team MUST be ready. Call your marketing manager in and ensure this person implements and executes a system of notifications on your social media platforms, so that the voices handling your two-way comm platforms respond to whatever comm they pick up from the audience. To make an example: if they do not respond within 3 minutes on Twitter; if they do not respond within 30 minutes on Facebook, or 10-15 minutes on LinkedIn, FIRE them! If your Webmaster does not respond to a respondable comment on your blog, or to some or other review, or whatever, wherever there is a comm directed at your business, grind their stinking balls! You have my permission, and Sun Tzu's blessings too.

Timeous, speedy response! Did you know there is an analytic that has been incorporated into Facebook Insights – response time? If you do not respond to your customer speedily, giving them the info they need, handling their complaints, acknowledging their compliments and so forth, then you WILL lose that prospect for good. And your competition will get the business you would have, could have; don't be stupid.

Customer service, is vital! That's just one component though of your time management policy. You also have to look at the timing of your posts and updates. Timing and frequency, that is.

As in military war, the general knows when to withhold fire, and when he orders FIRE! His troops send a hail of ammo until the signal comes to cease. Same on your social media platforms – posting updates and content, tweets, videos, etc. that's your ammo. Make sure you are well stocked for all occasions, but make sure these are timed well.

There's no hard or fast rules to timing your posts, especially if you're meting out a barrage of boosted posts on Facebook say. I stipulate this because the algorithm works different on paid posts than on organic ones. Paid ones will be shown to your networks at optimal times determined by the network. However, if you opt for pure organic reach, know this: one, you will not get as much reach in such a short space of time; and two, you will have to time your post better, which of course can be gauged through your analytics. More about this later, but for now, just let the idea sink in about timing your posts or updates.

What you want is to post something when most of your customers/prospects/followers/leads – call them what you want at this stage – are online; or rather *likely* to be online.

Think about your average workday – people get to the office what time? What do they do: grab some coffee, power up their pc, report in to management, and then hit the graft. Right, most hop online for a couple of minutes, browse all platforms, check their emails, you know the workforce seems to get this pretty rote these days. So, whatever time you work out they're likely to be on, make sure your post is scheduled for then. Same goes for mid-morning tea break, lunch time, mid afternoon tea break, after work; dinner times general activity seems to pitch on most networks in any event, and anywhere up to say 8ish pm. Weekends appear to have different routines and timing schedules, so, just put some brain into your timing.

And of course, you want to put some posts in between peak times or sweet spots, because not everyone is online at the same time.

There are two schools of thought, maybe a third, that I've taken note of on social media networks regarding best times to post. One school of thought says post a max of 2 posts daily on Facebook, 1 update on LinkedIn daily, and 6-8 tweets during the day on Twitter. Instagram, do a minimum of 1 upload per day. Pinterest, pin 2-3 things daily to your boards. Google Plus at least 1 daily. You get the picture. Adherents of this system say if you post more than that you'll be spamming and blocked and make more real enemies rather than followers you can engage with.

Then there's another school of thought that says, fuck that: your post is lost in someone's feed and so will only be seen the minute they're on, and they won't scroll down far in their feeds to see you either. So, their idea is always to be seen so your customers are constantly reminded you're there, you do x, you got y, you offer z ... Get it? And if you're labelled spamming, or blocked, SFW! There's hundreds of thousands more online to be targeted, and who don't have an issue, so get with the program.

The third school of thought generally believe in developing and maintaining a niche base of followers, they opt for quality over quantity, and so tend never to grow. They've always got the same people responding to stuff, and end up as boring as hell.

Like I say, no hard and fast rules here, but one thing is for sure whichever program you find works for you, do it. I prefer a blend between the first two schools of thought. Blitzing posts and updates when there are events or special things happening, and cooling it when things are like just normal, you know. Whatever, you HAVE TO keep posting something on a daily basis to these platforms.

Consistency and frequency is key for timing. The ability to be there, whenever, however is just as key. With today's technological means at your disposal there is absolutely no reason why you cannot respond to something 12 at night, or 2 am if need be. Generally, no asshole is going to do that to you, but given our time zones and global environment in cyberspace, the possibility *does* exist for your company in Johannesburg to get a response from some prick sitting in Sydney at a goddamn hour! Or even from LA for that matter, so just work around it.

Your voices online, the voices behind the voices ... those in your social media team ... they can knock off at 4-30 or 5 whatever yanks their chain; hell, they can even rock up at 8-30 or 9 for all I care. They have smartphones, tablets, 3G, whatever. If their notification buzzes activity requiring response on their device, they can fucken respond! There's no freaking excuse. Even if they pull that millennial shit, and want to go have a blast at the lake, or a coffee shop, or a friend's house, whatever – there's no excuse: they can go have all the fun they fucking want, but work is work, and they need to be responsible enough to deliver the barrage of responses needed when that device goes beep-beep! Get it.

Last thing to be said about timing – remember your competitors are watching you too! You're under the spotlight with them, so make no bones about it. Here's an example, I once did a tweet about some article. It was something quite arb to say the least. And I took a chance in posting it because I needed something to post, and had just run out of content (school fees learned, trust me!). Anyway, the article was about some method that was being used for something in 2015. And not having read the article properly, I did not realize that it was about a method that was last used in 2012, and had been phased out ever since. Next thing is several competitors out of the fucken blue, jumped on my timeline and made a farce of what I'd done. I worked the situation to my advantage though, and said something to the effect of pulling in engagement to my page, and thanks for noticing this deliberate blunder ... blah-blah-blah. Point is, these dudes and agencies like *never* engage with us, like *ever*. And here they were, jumping at my fuck-up. So, yeah, don't ever think they are not watching you!

Point I am making here, you can prolong your resources for the battle of gaining more followers, whilst your competitors are daily engaged in advertising and paying for reach and so forth. Or you can beat them to it, and blitz the market with things like new releases, new data, new things, new whatever. Works damn well in fashion, music, publishing, news, and related sectors, when there's always new things. Little different though for other sectors like health, insurance, services and so on.

If your competitor is posting an average of 3 updates a day; fuck him: you go ahead and post 4-5 a day! Get it: be better, be there! Use your ad spend for maximum effect, and grow your following base, and your influence rapidly. Chances are, your competitor will see these small advances and think you will not make it. Show them wrong.

Rapid fire your content, with effective messaging, carefully tailored to get them; and efficient use of both time and resources with the types of content developed … this will do the trick. If your business needs to deliver something the customer has purchased online – come hell or high water, get it to them without any delay, as fast as possible. Be better than your competition. Dominate the game.

Timing. Get, make and enforce this policy to the present participle of speed.

Policy #3: Strengthen yourself with each win

Now here's a thing you got to do to your staff in the frontline. Check out what the Master says about this:

> *So what kills the enemy is anger, what gets the enemy's goods is reward.*
> *Therefore, in a chariot battle, reward the first to capture at least ten chariots.*
> *Change their colours; use them mixed in with your own. Treat the soldiers [and prisoners of war] well, take care of them.*

> *This is called overcoming the opponent and increasing your strength to boot.*

Your sales team and your marketing team are supposed to work in unison on this. You need to see what will work best for your company. Personally I recommend Twitter for fast rapid sales, where your sales guy is tweeting and hooks onto a prospect who has shown interest. It's up to this guy to see how to run things. He may sell on the platform, or he may be able to get the lead onto another platform, like email, or simply meet the prospect in person and convert the lead into business.

I have to say this about lead conversion. Digital media – that is, the internet, your website, email and social media is designed for you to convert the lead *digitally*. Digital conversion can never replace physical conversion. By this I mean, it is most of the time way better to meet the prospect in person. The closest may be a video call via whichever relevant medium if distance and time does not permit otherwise; but the best way to convert someone is always in person, face-to-face. You see, it makes it very real when someone is face to face with you. Here you will find truth; whereas digitally people can always be cowards and back off from a deal. So, you have to use digital to get their digital details and then physically close the prospect on whatever you are selling them.

There's many instances of this, and I have personal experience with this ranging from selling people books and fashion garments, to handling government accounts where a certain Trade and Industry body was prospecting the market for foreign direct investment. I am not at liberty to say for which government here). Being their online voice, as in responding to online comments, queries, and so on, I found myself in the position one day with a query from an FDI qualified prospect worth a few billion dollars at the end of the day. The comment came in response to a stream of content we had posted. This guy was from the UAE (Dubai). He left a comment on a post on LinkedIn asking for an email and more info. The client was too late to respond and so I intercepted the comm, went into the prospects profile, he had no contacts listed, but I could see he was amply qualified to make good on an investment that the government body needed. So, in order to get this guy, I went onto Twitter and searched for him, eventually found some egg-head handles, and went through several until I found the right one. Then I tweeted the guy and DM'd him. In the meantime, I found other info on his Twitter bio that enabled me to piece together how to contact this guy on Facebook, and again I in-boxed him there too.

Within hours the guy responded on Twitter, and we got chatting. Long story short, he was aboard a flight to London, and I got his number and the right person from our clients' office then got in touch with him and took the deal further. You see, now the client had expended some budget on daily posts for a campaign run purely off Facebook, and if they closed this lead, what would that have been worth both to their internal team, and to the agency running their campaign? And, as you guessed it, they were like super-amped for the next campaign. So amped their CEO ordered more budget be allocated to marketing. There was real ROI! Get it.

And as for our agency running the show, they were amply rewarded so could employ better resource in the form of a graphic designer to spice things up a notch and create better graphics for the updates across all the platforms. In other words, the win-win meant that everyone benefited internally. The company strengthened its marketing endeavours to be better able to deliver better in future. In fact, our agency won an Industry Award for our integrated marketing campaign, in which the client had grown from 1.4 billion to 3.7 billion over an 18-month campaign!

The rewards I am talking about here are more to bolster the morale of your team. That can be done on a gradient scale of several factors. Set them targets like follower counts; numbers of posts and conversations had. That will force these fuckers to engage from the brand to the public. And that my friend is the only way you are going to build relationships, is with engagement.

What is engagement? Talking online. Not just hi, how the fuck are you stuff! Couldn't give a shit about that stuff. Talk about their interests; them; what are they doing; what is their opinion about abc? What solutions do they offer? You get it? Real conversations man, like I would have with someone I met at a conference, or did a cold call to, or bump into at the mall. Reward your team, if not financial incentive for the time being, do it with trophies of recognition or something to make them feel that whatever they are doing is valuable.

It's all too easy to pump content out and ... fuck, I've been there man. Let me tell you something, if you get no feedback from that General steering you and ordering you to FIRE! You feel like you're engaged in a thankless fucking routine and monotonous job. Right, so you want to avoid your frontline staff ever thinking along those lines. Order them pizza out of the blue to celebrate wins. *Something*, you know, come on, I don't have to teach you leadership skills now as well. If you don't they may eventually end up blowing from the post, and deserting your frontline. And the replacement cost of someone in the know of your processes, standards, clients, customers, competitors, etc. ... you don't get to replace that overnight. Don't be stupid! Nurture what you got, and you will even find these peeps will go hogs more for you and your brand.

I've seen them blow. I've seen them blow, disconnect and block themselves from your brand. I've seen them fuck right over to your competitor, or having learned all your secrets, leaving you to go it alone and become direct fucking competition to you! There's no restraint of trade that will keep this motherfucker down. There's always a way. So, look after what you got, and reward them to strengthen yourself even further.

Policy #4: Know your stuff

The issue of leadership is very pertinent in policy. Remember in the beginning I said your incumbent in the Social Media Management role – and call this what you like too, some call it Community Manager, others call it Social Lead, whatever – this person MUST be a leader in the true sense. This is the general on the ground who must handle the contingencies and field budgets and direct their team to certain actions.

This person MUST know their stuff!

They have to have expert knowledge and practice of every facet of social media and digital marketing there is. They have to be able to see straight through the bullshit. They have to see the bigger picture with all the detail. If you must, send them on training for this and that to sharpen them; this is in your best interests too.

In fact, the whole team or anyone involved in any facet of your social media and digital marketing efforts. Get them trained, chiseled man. Sharpened. They cannot waste time on the battle grounds figuring out how to create a profile for a client; or how to respond to a complaint, or fuck around with appropriateness of words and the like. They cannot be negligent to miss out on opportunities as they present themselves, or to slacken on the quality control of posts and graphics. They cannot waste time figuring out how to work a new feature that has been upgraded on the platform either, or miss out on the trends.

When last did you do a Friday Follow on Twitter – you know - #FF – huh? When last did you do a SHOUTOUT to abc? No, forgotten about these things because they have fallen out of use already! So, you get the point – know your stuff so you stay current. Follow the trends. People love the trends. Remember the Ice-Bucket challenge, and I nominate blah! Remember the rainbow campaign on your profile pic; and the semi-colon campaign in support of counter-suicide measures? You have to be in the loop with current news, trends and so on, especially where these are things that have a direct impact on your particular industry.

Stay current, stay in the loop. Know your stuff, policy #4.

Launch Strategic Attacks

Ok, quick recap: you've got your initial assessment done. You've profiled your typical online customer. You've got a SWOT analysis done. You've done a thorough competitors analysis, and you pretty much know the market now. You know your customer. You know your competitors. You know the digital landscape, where you need to be, and present your Calls to Action. And now, you've just developed a policy with which to go to war. So let's focus on the strategic attack zones. How are you going to *execute* your strategy?

Win Online Customers without a Fight

What are we trying to achieve by having profiled your ideal customer? Well, the best strategy to have is never to react to your competitor. It's a free market economy. React to your competitor and you will land in some serious litigation and courthouse shit. Trust me, you don't need that shit in your life! Anyway, it's a battle to obtain customers and to dominate your space. You want all your competitor's customers to come to you. So, what we're doing here is defining the opportunity at which to strike; or in other words, defining the opportunity at which to win your customers.

Another thing about strategy – a paradox if you like, by Sun Tzu – its not to kill in confrontation. You want to show power, so the enemy shits themselves and gives in before anything escalates. Only here, we're not talking about anyone "shitting themselves", in the fearful sense of the expression. Your customers need to storm onto your digital platforms to get your offering as it will be something pleasurable for them, not done out of fear. Although I suppose if you must, you could say they would be afraid not to have your product. #witnation, lol. Whatever, let's not get our balls all jangled in the semantics of things. It's the principle here, and your strategy needs to add value for them to follow you. You need to have something better than your competitors.

In the wars of Sun Tzu's time, the idea was to capture territory intact, so the resources and population can be plundered and enjoyed. It's about capturing wealth. Not fucking something up, or plundering it so that you have to spend money to fix it up all over again. You want to capture your enemy's wealth, make it your own. So, now you know who they are – your customers and competitors, and what they've got in general terms.

Next thing you need to do is win this war without fighting. But isn't war about fighting? Of course it is. Use your head stupid. Fight with your head! It's about superiority and domination, you see. They come running when they see they cannot fight against you.

Why is it that you like the Nike brand page on your Facebook, but you don't even wear Nike? Or you like CNN news, but you never watch it? Or National Geographic is cool but you watch all the stupid little kitty vines instead? It's because these are powerful brands man. You know the brand name. It's a household name. You like it, because you've seen it, heard about it. Everyone likes it, and you don't want to be the odd one out. You understand.

A profiled customer is what you are after here. Talk to a lower LSM about MacDonald's and Burger King. Talk to an upper LSM about boutique restaurants and cuisine. LSM is Living Standards Measurement. You get the point. They're all your customers, but some won't afford you, so waste them.

What you are doing in targeting your profiled customer is you are capturing market share and dominance against your competition. And before they know it, you will have their customers ... and their business. You see, Sun Tzu was a very clever man. Check out what Sun Tzu says here:

> *Those who win every battle are not really skillful – those who render others' armies helpless without fighting are the best of all.*
>
> *The superior militarist strikes while schemes are being laid. The next best is to attack alliances. The next best is to attack the army.*
>
> *One who is good at martial arts [warfare] overcomes others' forces without battle, conquers others' cities without siege, destroys others' nations without taking a long time.*

So, to capture market share without assaulting the competitor, in essence, is to indirectly put them out of business through targeting the correct customer.

It's no use having done a competitor's analysis and doing exactly what your competitor is doing – unless of course they are already weaker than you online. This is especially true if you are new to social media and digital marketing and seeking an entry point to the market domain.

By this I mean, you now take a look at your competitor's analysis and again size things up versus what you know about your online customer. You see your competitors – A gets their market in through quotes and gimmick posts. B gets their following from jokes and product info. C gets them in using cool pics and shared articles. D does this and E does that. Some of them copy each other. Yet, they're all selling the same thing. You may find C has the highest following, but in terms of business A is the stronger brand. And here you want to break into that market and gain dominance. So, what's your plan?

Like I say, sizing up all the factors, you may find your market entry tactic through holding a competition. Or something different, whilst giving them info and showing your strengths through friendly real customer service online. Then it's just a matter of moving swiftly so as to establish yourself and put you on the map.

Be sure to win once you have done everything up to now. Your competitors are smug and gloating, thinking they cannot be taken on line. Sure, they may have even been there for 5, 6, 7 years already; and it's taken them long to build their following. All the more reason for them not to become so complacent. Their customers, their followers are by now probably so fucking bored that they will jump at new innovations, novelties and things.

Sun Tzu says that you only win battles with concentrated strengths. How does this apply to targeting customers and eliminating competition? One word:

Budgets.

That's right. Ad spend, advertising budget. You want to advertise your stuff online where your customer is located.

How do you ensure your competition who may have more ad spend will not sideline you with their own ad campaign? My answer again – your competitor's analysis, with accent on your SWOT must highlight where the strengths and weaknesses lay – because these translate into your opportunities and threats. Develop your strengths where your competitor shows weakness.

Let me give you an example. A client of ours, in the recruitment and staffing sector entered online markets with absolutely zero brand presence whatsoever. We did the initial assessment and discovered who their competitors were. Then we did a competitors' analysis and discovered their biggest competitor had a huge brand presence on LinkedIn and Facebook, but not much on Twitter. We also discovered the other competitors were very small on Facebook and Twitter, but big on LinkedIn. Yeah, yeah, yeah, my client cheered – let's whack it out on LinkedIn!

Now, yes and no. Yes, let's put you on LinkedIn, but no, don't waste budget on LinkedIn ads for the time being until we have a much bigger following. We decided to throw resource onto Facebook and Twitter, and within no time at all had grown their Twitter to significantly dominate the space, so much so that the only way their competitor would be able to catch up would be to buy followers, which are a waste of time as these are not pre-qualified or authentic users of the market products anyway. And we hammered the comm lines with updates and tweets, obtained good engagement too. Then we implemented a few short campaigns to drive traffic between the platforms, so that at the end of the day our LinkedIn presence automatically grew, with no resource spent on LinkedIn advertising. In as little as a year, the brand had gone from complete obscurity to the second best player in the market for that recruitment niche, and is now poised to become the top leader in the market within the following 4-6 months by my calculation.

You see, Sun Tzu works, my friends. Concentrate your strengths where the enemy is weak, and hammer away in short decisive victories on those fronts to gain ground. When eventually the competitors saw what we were doing, they quickly tried to fight similar campaigns of their own on Twitter and Facebook, but we had taken them by surprise. They had very little skilled social media teams to get them from A-Z on Twitter, and threw resource at getting themselves up to speed; to the point that some of those competitors had contacted our company to give them training so they could improve themselves. Which is fine, once they have been trained, the client had by then more than doubled its current capacity and market share. So good luck fuckers!

Attack where your enemy is weak. If it's your competitors, attack where they are weak and vulnerable. When it's your customer find their weakness, where they *cannot* say no. You will find this through profiling them.

Lead your Marketing and Sales Team

Now, let's assume the game is on. You're in action, and your social media team is following, posting, responding to comments and monitoring your competition. The truth is these guys are your troops. Word of advice – don't be an asshole to them.

So, you're the big shot CMO/CIO/Creative Director – whatever whoever you are, right. You think it's your prerogative to monitor them. Sure it is, you're the general steering those troops. But I bet you your eyes are not on them all the time. And it needn't be. You have so much other executive responsibilities on your plate, right. So, something happens like you discover black PR and you react to it. Delete a few posts because you have admin rights and order the social media manager to issue this statement and that. Or tell them to take things down or put other things up, etc. What you're doing is creating more confusion. If you've already got your policy in place, your social media team will know how to respond, and do you proud at the end of the day. Be the general and remain the general, otherwise take a demotion to corporal and go fight on the frontlines with them.

#justsaying #rantover #dontbestupid

Got it? Avoid acting without full knowledge about the situation your marketing is in. Avoid micromanaging your social media team, your marketing team. You cannot hope to have any competent marketers on your team if you get into all their details.

We had a disastrous incident once, just to quickly illustrate this. We were monitoring the social media pages for a listed recruitment company. The company had implemented an aggressive marketing campaign, which included radio, TV, billboards, magazines, newspapers, as well as social media. In fact the social media component was simply going to be a support instrument within the greater publicity run of things. Well there we were, merrily going about our daily duties as an agency. When suddenly a message appeared on Twitter from some motorist showing their disgust at a billboard notice alongside the highway. The billboard alluded to career suicide if you as a candidate failed to do anything about looking for a job, and so the motorist turned into a digital troll and took things out of context about the brand advocating suicide.

So, this was reported up-lines and the general ontop was enraged – how dare the fucking client do this to our agency! Lol – the client had authorized what their billboard marketer, a specialist in that field had recommended for them. Anyway, the general hops on the phone to the Marketing Director of the client – you see! We told you if you do something controversial what will happen, now the whole of the fucking town has seen the billboard and it's going to damage your brand: they now think you want job seekers to commit suicide!

Ok dudes, it's okay to get silent on me like that. So what happened next? General gets the client to issue a PR statement in agreement with the troll and issues orders to have the billboard taken down within the next few days.

In the meantime, the PR has gone viral. Troll deluxe is now on a glory campaign in town - check it out, I'm the main ape man! This chick – she was a chick troll – lets the city council, the top radio stations and news media in on this; and of course her following and everyone goes ape shit on Twitter. How dare the client advocate suicide! You get what happened?

Do yourself a favor and go back to the beginning of the story here and re-read what I said. I said an analogy had been made on the billboard between career suicide and not doing anything about your situation as a job seeker. Get it? Nothing in the message *actually* advocated suicide. It was very intelligent marketing, not some dumb-ass stupid slap dash message put up. And I told the General, as a strategist, that we could do far more by using what was perceived to be controversy than what had happened.

You see how easy it is for things to get pulled out of context on social media? We could actually have made more out of keeping the perceived controversy alive than getting the client to take their boards down. Don't even ask how much money they lost in having to take the boards down. Needless to say, that General also lost their client a month later because they had no balls. My advice was to keep the boards up and run public debate on the topic of suicide and through media awareness the troll would have been exposed as dumbass for not understanding the message as well as her followers who would have deserted her and joined our ranks.

The last thing you need to do before executing your strategy is to GET your people to GO to battle. Dispose of your strengths, in military terms. This means – your marketing and sales team need to be operationalized. You need to put your social media team, your Webmaster, your advertisers and digital marketers if you outsource to them, into the firing lines on the battlefield. They need to be empowered as brand ambassadors to be able to speak on behalf of your company, to be your voice. To respond to customers, to reach for customers, to use their initiative to fight to conquer and bring victory to your brand. And this should at some point, somehow translate into money in the bank.

This is where we can now look at how you will manage these troops on the battleground, so that you can send orders now and then to change this or do that. You understand; war is a fluid medium of negotiations. Your enemy is subject to many tactics and counter-tactics and you need to be ready for any of these things.

I'm not going to get into the detail of these things you should be doing, because that will be entering the realm of tactics and tactical warfare, which will depend solely on the expert training of your team, and the initiative they use to do things.

Here I just want you as the leader of your brand to understand strategy and the macro-mindset needed to see the big picture and win. The only details that should be of concern to you is the analytics and reports you need to receive, that is to say, the intelligence from which you can steer things.

A good friend of mine has a brilliant social media strategy to market his books online. He did some sales, but they were insignificant. He let the platform run its gamut for about 6 months, before coming to the conclusion his resources were being wasted in content that was not doing the trick; and that although he had a significant following base, especially on Twitter, these were not really the right followers who would actually reach for his books; many being located within the same genre in any event. So we simply wasted it. Nuked it. Stopped his social media daily activities instantly.

And you know what? He had resource now to throw at mailers from his website, sprucing up his mailing list with latest books and info to followers who could now click directly through to Amazon and Kindle to do their purchases. And he got the sales he was after in the first place.

So, again, Sun Tzu shows not to waste time on strengths – go for the weaknesses. On social media, this publisher came to dominate the landscape – so had placed themselves in positions of strength. By now attacking the weaknesses – the crappy website that got overhauled, and establishing a mailer system there, he reached success.

What's the moral of this story? Don't be afraid to waste something if it is not working. Digital marketing works – wherever it is volleyed at weakness. You need to be where your customer is. You need to make it as easy as possible for your customer to do business with you. You need to be so attractive an option amidst your competitors that it will be a really easy choice – and don't give them that choice. Hook them, suck them in, keep them, make them addicted to your products and services that they will come for more and more and more, and bring their friends and family and …

You get the points raised in this section – give your troops on the frontlines the scope to decide for themselves the best lines of action to deal with things. They deal with such things daily, and so get to know the lines in a different way than the General does.

Know when to obey the rules of engagement. These are also part of policy, but need to be expanded on, so I have decided to address these in a separate chapter.

PART 3

RULES OF ENGAGEMENT

Apply Rules of Engagement to Social Sales

All this talk about engagement ... how are you feeling right now? Hyped up and ready to do whatever it takes?

What is engagement anyway?

In military terms, when you engage the enemy, you pretty much confront him, open fire, fuck the shit out of him, and seize what you wanted. Sound crass? Good. It's survival of the fittest man. War is just a means to an end. If you're not fighting to kill or be killed, you're maybe not doing it with violence, but let me tell you, whatever you use – mind, heart, soul, whatever – the object is conquest and plunder.

It's a universal rule. You want to survive, love ain't going to do it. You want to survive; manners and being all nice and considerate ain't going to cut the grade either. You want it make a plan and go fucken get it! It's as simple and as easy as that. You are at war!

Every minute, every second of the day, when you wake up, when you close your eyes, you are at war against something. Something: it can be your own thoughts, your cells are fighting off infections, bacteria and crap; your morality is staving off evil, you're pushing for those sales, you're pushing for those customers, you're pushing to fucking survive ... and if you're going to be a fucking pussy about it, you are dead! Dead man. And all your dependents with you! Dead fucken dead! Am I making my point here?

You are at war! Think like Sun Tzu. Think survival and conquest. Think life, and what you can have by surviving, because if you think anything else you are going to die hungry, miserable, worse than a dog. And nobody cares; nobody gives a shit about you when you're dead. Much less when you are alive, so you have to rise from those ashes that are holding you as a prisoner to death and just fucking fly man.

Fight now!

Rules of engagement.

In digital marketing those same military rules Sun Tzu wrote about apply to this day! Read them, learn them, know them, apply them, and win! Let me list these for you:

> *So there are five ways of knowing who will win.*
>
> 1. *Those who know when to fight and when not to fight are victorious.*
> 2. *Those who discern when to use many or few troops are victorious.*
> 3. *Those whose upper and lower ranks have the same desire are victorious.*
> 4. *Those who face the unprepared with preparation are victorious.*
> 5. *Those whose generals are able and are not constrained by their governments are victorious.*
>
> *These five are the ways to know who will win.*

Note that in a similar quotation above, Sun Tzu spoke of the assessments for comparison as being the ways in which you will know who can win. This reference now takes that dimension further, because you've by now done your strategic assessment in the form of a full competitors' analysis. Now not only will you know who *can* win, but with these five factors, you will know who *WILL WIN*.

So, what does this mean in the rules of engagement? By the way, engagement, ironically, is a digital marketing analytic that factors in the number of likes, comments, and shares divided by your followers. It is very measurable. That means it is in itself a source of intel for the General. It will tell you how many people you shot to put it quite bluntly. Reach on the other hand, when advertising or promoting your post, especially, is an extended form of your engagement. This is where you nuke them – a whole bunch of them – those who are out of range of your present battlefield, where you have only contact through engagement. Reach is the sum of all your followers who mention your brand by way of simply having liked you, plus the sum of all *their* followers. So, you see, their followers need not be present engaging with you – but you can still reach them by tracing the networks of those engaged with you. And this is where the magic of social media comes in – because cyberspace through algorithms, edge rank, and all of those fancy mechanisms, gets those networks faster than you can even type the instruction!

What Sun Tzu is saying, is it is extremely probable you will fail at your marketing efforts and in business if you ignore these rules that will guarantee success. It's just a handful of principles to live by here. Let me unpack it further for you in the next chapters.

Success Begins with Intel

Think about it for a sec. I mean in the 50+ pages above, we've been looking at info gathering, intel systems culminating in your competitor's analysis. So, I cannot stress this point enough – organize and develop your intelligence system so that you know your market like the palm of your hand. Got it? Now part of all the mammoth data you need to study, is your analytics – not just your observations of the market place. You have to put your attention on *your* analytics, because when things are data-driven, man, I tell you, you can fuck them up and succeed!

Intelligence is the ability to draw conclusions through both observation and inference (or deduction, depending how you examine the data); and the decision on a suitable course of action to either react or respond to a situation.

I will devote a separate chapter to the analytics below. For now, suffice it that you have analytics for anything in cyberspace. Your website enjoys Google Analytics, social media – they all have their own accessible metrics to make light of what's happening. There is no excuse – many of these analytic platforms are free as well. Of course, you can jump onto Social Bakers, or Hubspot, or Simply Measured for comprehensive cross-platform analytics at a premium – nice to have these things all centralized in an already established organizational system for your data. Or you can just pop onto the individual metric platforms for targeted analytics. This will all depend on your budget. There's no excuse not for having access to your analytics though, budget or not.

Maintain Your Objectives

Be sure what you are doing online. If you are expanding your following, don't get sidelined with being told you are spamming them, or overdoing your content. There's no such thing. You cannot please everyone. In any event, when attacking with content as your ammo, I have yet to see the other side flag you as firing too much! Your followers have the power to block, mute, or disconnect from you invariably. Most probably will never do so; and good riddance to those that do! So, yes, fire away baby!

A client of mine once held back on expansion because some fucknut phoned in and told him if he receives one more email about his product he will go to court, and can he please be removed from the database. Yeah sure, we nuked the bastard! But then the client said, hey I am scared now, I cannot afford another customer to come and take offence. And that was that client done for! Worst month of sales ever, when he could have gone really big.

You have to be willing to waste some followers. Treat them like rotten apples. All the apples you harvest, once on the sorting table get sifted anyway, and the obviously rotten ones are thrown out. Same thing here, folks.

Keep the customer happy in this sense? Fuck the customer dude! That's right, give them freebies and smiles, and waste your budget on them never buying from you. Uh-uh. Think again – you are at war. No more Mr. Nice Guy. One person and you think it's the end?

You have nothing to prove to keep a happy customer who never buys. Nuke them! You don't need that! You need someone who will buy! Or at least who is willing to stay interested until eventually they buy. You get the point. Don't lose the objective. Be clear on what you want. We're so worried about reporting platforms like hellopeter.com and being reported to the platform administrator, for what and why? Remember this: you have freedom of action to maneuver, and don't let anybody stop you!

Nothing stopped Nicole Arbour! You see she's a YouTuber, selling her comedy. Some really borderline humor there, and she got taken down because some people found a video highly offensive – you know, the one about Fat People; and the other one about Jesus; and so what! If the customer doesn't like it, hey, they have the power to unfollow, block and go back into their own shells. No problem. Don't ever be hard up for customers. So, what happened? YouTube left her down for a few days and then put her back up, and her following doubled over fucking night! You know how many gigs she got now? Pesky handful of bitches and pricks that took offence should just have stayed off the platform and exercised their own rights of association. They were never forced to view her videos in any event. So, like I said … good riddance!

You get the point. People have been dulled into a sense of complacency about the socially acceptable thing. And you will find those people screaming loudest are all guilty of shit themselves –

hell, they jump on pornhub.com and redtube.com! They snoop and troll as and when it suits them! Don't be sidelined from your objective. You will be surprised how much support you actually have out there.

Establish a Secure Position

Look, nothing is ever secure. You win some, you lose some. So, that's not the security I am talking about here. We are interested in getting yourself, your company, your brand, into a position of strength where your competitor cannot take you on. So, how do you do that? Short answer: be better than them! Beat them on every front imaginable. Just get ahead of them.

Your marketing team – make sure they are top caliber, well-trained on all the digital platforms they need to be on – and I am talking everything from Skype, to webinars, to social media and how to use Photoshop for what it is worth. They need to be kick-ass or you need to be kicking their asses. One of the two.

Get more followers than your enemies. Pump more content than them. Offer bigger prizes, better discounts, whatever it takes for you to be better, just do it, okay. Secure your position so well, that when they land on your platform they are in, man, they can't get out unless they close the fucking browser – you understand! And of course make the ride one they will totally enjoy.

That much said, get rid of all the shit in your network too. Get the negative people off your lines, wherever they are. Get the trolls out. Get the naysayers and critics the fuck away from what you're doing – both in your following, and in your team. Nuke them! Don't worry about numbers here. Only good can come from good things and good energy, and good vibes.

I need to bring something to your attention, and this pertains to your website here. I have seen so many websites with this fundamental problem, and it is committed by 2 kinds of people all the time. The first person is your stupid Webmaster or web-designer who's just treating you as their client and another job. They have no pride in their work, no strategic foresight either. The second person is the strategist recommending what should be done, because they just don't get this. So what are they doing? They're not enabling strategic links to open within your website.

But all my links open! Really? Are you sure about that? Here's the low down. They may open all right, but they are not all opening *within* your website, in such a way that will keep the customer *in* your domain. You see, especially with YouTube links. What happens? I click on your video, nice, very nice. It's too small for my liking, and there's a little tab there that says I can open it in YouTube where I can see it in a bigger scale. So I click, what happens? YouTube opens! Done with the video, I close the window and want to go back, only to find I just closed the whole browser and now have to search for your company again. By that time, I'm like tired and my attention has been caught by something else, and bam! You've just lost me!

Your link to anything in your website MUST open in a separate tab in my browser. That way, when I am done and close the tab, I find I am still in your site! And hey, something else has caught my eye and now you got my attention, and I'm going to click around to satisfy my curiosity, and each click is your chance to convert me; and get me further interested, and reaching for more, like I just have to HAVE your products and services somehow. When I'm done on your site, I need to be talking to you asking things like how, much, where, when?

If you have social media icons on your website pages, make sure they work and take me straight through to your pages. Get it? Secure your position so I cannot escape. Make it memorable for me.

Some websites I see have a little feature that if you try to close the browser or open a new page, or even click away, you get a pop-up to choose whether or not you wish to leave the page or stay on it. Now, you don't need this kind of feature on every page – just on the substantive pages that are designed to close a prospect. You should in any event have done everything possible to by now have at least obtained the visitors' email address, that you can use at a later stage in database format for email marketing, and so on.

Right; secure your position online.

BE on and STAY on the OFFENSIVE

Maintain a continuous systematic attack on your enemy. This is a daily activity. Always move forward, even if it's one follower per day (although that is really not acceptable, when you should be getting hundreds and thousands daily). Tell me something; does a soldier sleep while fighting? Need I answer that for you? So, why are you or your team not responding to customers the minute they engage with you online?

Get this: a customer sends you an online request for blah, and after an hour or two feels ignored. What's happened here? He shot you with an "I want some info" bullet. You never responded. So the message the customer got was, the fucker is dead! Let's go find someone else to shoot. Got it? You cannot afford to die! You got to fight him back until you win with your "buy my product" bullet.

Always be on the offensive – and do not give a damn about who is offended by it! Fuck them, they are losers, not surviving, and all they are screaming is "I'm hurt, your bullet has wounded me". So what do you do? Nuke them! Shut them up. Take no such prisoners.

Offensive does not mean in this sense to be offensive, as in offending people intentionally. I mean, it's okay to be controversial and do whatever to draw attention, ethically of course. I mean don't go engage in hate speech to draw attention. Offensive here means to be vigilantly pursuing more followers. You know, broadening your horizons, vigorously expanding your network. There's no shortage of followers in the world out there. Think about this: there's over 7-billion peeps on this planet. They're not all online, but those that are comprise almost 4-billion at the time I am writing this book. In your country, wherever you are, I am sure there alone you have a good couple of million followers to pursue.

So, there's no shortage of followers online. Followers – aka prospects, customers, leads, sales, money!!!

Surprise Them

Your announcements, the info and news you share, those new product releases, competitions, these must all speak to surprising both your online prospect and your competitor.

Announce you have just made huge sales amidst the recession, when you know your competitors are failing. Gain psychological dominance, and use this to your advantage.

You know all those motivational gurus' who use The Secret, right? *Energy goes where attention flows*. You know the adage, right? Use that here. Surprise them by drawing attention to your victories. Show them you are expanding and growing, and doing well. Get them to hate you with venom. They need to spit and froth at the mouth every time they see you in cyber-space.

Ah yes, the haters. Love your haters. These folks are gold. Really! Just think about the dynamics of a hater for a sec. What does a hater do? A hater voices how much they don't like you, or accuse you of this and that, right? Yet, so many supporters think and feel differently about you. And a hater draws attention; so actually they work for you in a certain sense. You don't even have to engage with them; they're like people who have been shot in an ambush out in the field, and they scream drawing attention to exactly where the fight is.

You know what I am saying – surprise them.

Announce new thought, new views, new perspectives on your industry. Announce whatever will draw more attention when things are down. Stay positive of course, no negativity.

Manoeuvre into a Position of Strength

Be clever – be vigilant and use your savvy. Use your head. Look for any opportunity to strike. Your competitor just launched a new service. Launch something better. Your competitor failed to give answers, intercept and give answers. A prospect just posted an update: they need xyz. Pitch up with it! Always be maneuvering to be better, know more, do more, have more, and give more.

Whoever said you cannot go on your competitors' page and post comments? Nobody! Plus, this is the age of networking and social media. This is the digital age, where we are interconnected. You need to take advantage of this fact. If you notice your competitor is not responding to prospects online, why not engage their prospects on their own pages? If somebody has asked a question, and the competitor has not answered; why not go on and answer the prospect. In all likelihood, the competitor most probably would not even notice you have done so; and here's the thing: who do you think the prospect will respond to? Your competitor? No way dude! They will respond to you, because you keep it real. When next your competitor looks, you will have closed the deal on their page!

Play the attention game with surprise. Just do it. Making sense here? Exploit any and all of each of your competitors' weaknesses and vulnerabilities routinely to put yourself in a better advantage with which to capture more and more business.

Concentrate Resources, Focus Strengths

Whatever you do on social media, especially, do it fucking well. If you're running a campaign – run it, do not get distracted with trivialities and arbitraries. Remember you have budget – do not waste it. Do not create a scenario where you will have to waste it either. And do not create a situation where you may send conflicting messages to your audience. Stay focused on particular objectives until you have completed them.

Economy of Force is the Governing Principle

This is pretty much the corollary of concentrating resources to be strong. But remember you do not have capacity maybe to control the entire field of operations. So, what happens is, you strengthen yourself on one platform for example, and then find you are weak on another. This happened to us with a government trade sector client. We built them huge on Twitter - because that's where their biggest competitor was. And whilst we gained stride, that competitor focused their efforts on building their Facebook following, and when we looked again, we dominated the Twitter landscape, but lost ground on Facebook. Now, that was ok, because we were in any event leagues ahead on Facebook; and ran a series of Facebook campaigns after our Twitter stunt to regain ground and dominance. As for our competitor, they had by now exhausted their budget and so we got to dominate two fronts. Get it? Be clever again, but know whatever action you take will leave you weak in another area.

You don't have sufficient budget for LinkedIn ads and sponsored posts? Don't let that hold you back; use what you have. Maximize your manipulation of organic reach if you have insufficient budget. Know this, as long as you are doing something, you are making progress. It's when you stop doing things and hold back, that you lose ground. So, simply work smart with the resource and content at your disposal.

Keep it Simple and EARN with Social Sales

Your content must be easy to understand and comprehend. No need for complicated stuff. The last thing you want is a confused customer. Keep it simple so you can win. Don't use big fancy words and things that will take a thesaurus and encyclopedia to understand. And hey – that goes for all facets that we've been discussing above too. Take your analytics for example, when you analyze the figures and graphs and all that stuff, keep your insights simple too. And … the team you use, keep your goals, your aims and objectives, your targets, all that management and leadership stuff – keep it all simple and clear-cut. The moment things like messages, content, reporting, admin, communications and all that stuff gets complicated and complex, you are going to get nowhere. Keep it simple, real and easy to understand. You have one primary objective: get followers to want to buy your products and services. There's a whole lot of money there, folks!

Now, coming to social sales … here's the meat! You need to think like a customer approaching your brand. There's 2 things to bear in mind here. First, you're on social media. That means as a fan, a friend, a customer, a prospect, a lead, a follower, a visitor, a whatever-you-would-like to name this: you have the power of controlling the interaction online. Most people if they don't like something, they simply nuke you by clicking away or closing the tab or browser, and then you've almost lost them. Of course you can pursue them, locate them within social media and follow up. I've done that many times. Sometimes it paid off, other times it never paid off at all; and I got slammed with online harassment; which is okay – I only got a warning from the platform Help Centre. See the worry in my eye! It paid off oh so lucratively one occasion in particular, where I traced a prospective FDI donor for a client, and something actually came of it!

Secondly, you got the novelty in a prospect discovering a real voice behind the brand. Out of the sheer intrigue, they will communicate with you at first, especially where they are interested in what you have. This is the element I wish to focus on briefly here.

You see, a prospect is on your page because something has pulled their attention. Something you got in your content looks appealing enough for them to click through to engage. They comment – especially on Twitter and Facebook, and if you are right there the moment this happens, you can respond appropriately. I'm not talking about the following kind of conversation:

> *Prospect*: Wow! Love this garment of yours! (maybe they even share it to their own page).
> *Brand*: Thank you. Glad you love it ☺

I mean really now, folks! Is that all you can respond? You see, when it comes to social sales, you need to put on the salesman hat online. You're not a robot automating content. So, no need to automate a response. Keep it real. This is the kind of conversation you should be having:

Prospect: Wow! Love this garment of yours! (maybe they even share it to their own page).

Brand: Thank you. Glad you love it ☺ Bet it would look better on you. Why not visit our store and try one out for size?

Prospect: Oh no, I'm way over size for it. I was just saying it's a great looking design.

Brand: C'mon we got great clothes for all sizes. Tell you what, you come in and see us; why not bring a friend along too? We'll treat you to a free manicure, no obligations to buy anything.

Prospect: A free manicure? Wow! Don't know when last I had one of those!

Brand: Lol. ☺ Hey, you deserve it! When can we expect you?

Prospect: Hoo-boy, I'll have to ask my hubby.

Brand: That's ok. Why not surprise him?

Prospect: What do you mean?

Brand: You know … Come with your friend and you'll go home with gorgeous looking nails for free, yes?

Prospect: Hell yeah, it's about time I treated myself! Where about are you?

Brand: @Prospect [Whatever her handle name is], we're on the corner of 4th and Main. There is ample parking in the building if you're coming with your car.

Prospect: Wonderful! This is so exciting. I am so bringing Vanessa! We'll be there at 2.

Brand: Perfect @prospect! When you get here, just ask for Veronica, and she'll

> take care of you. We are delighted to have you.
>
> *Prospect*: Is it okay if I bring my other bestie?
>
> *Brand*: Ma'am, you bring as many bestie's as you got ☺

Get the point with a social sale? You have to seize the initiative. You have to take the sale by the horns and lead the conversation. Sure, you will lose some, and so what! The mere fact that you are getting this kind of engagement with your brand online, will most assuredly bring more prospects onto your platform. In the above conversation, I have really just simplified it to the basics here. You will notice there's been no hard sell online! There's been no question about prices. There's been no lying, manipulating, or underhanded things done! We have merely converted the prospect into a lead, to get them to our store for a face-to-face encounter with the sales staff who can take it further to close them, so we can bag a sale. You know, squeeze some cash out of them and water our bank!

This kind of comm-cycle is based on some or other post you did with content directed at your products and services. Let me illustrate another example now, wherein there's been no direct promo in your stream. I mean, to keep it real, social media is not just about hard-core content that slams the market with WE ARE XYZ; and WE OFFER ABC; and Get This and Buy Now! It's also about keeping it fun and light with relevant things that keep people interested. So, take a light-hearted post for example. I'm sure you've seen the post that asks you to look carefully at it and when you see it to like it, right? Now, there's going to be some prick that's just going to spoil it for everyone and let the cat out of the bag! So, we may have a conversation played by the brand as follows:

> *Prospect 1:* Ha-ha-ha ... wonder who the guy is in the background?

Prospect 2: Took me a while to see that!

Prospect 3: I had to zoom in to see it!

Prospect 4: What the ... that's impossible!

Prospect 1: Na, happened to me once. Was looking at a chick and walked straight into the pole!

Prospect 3: Yeah, but to leave a dent like that?

Brand: @Prospect 1 – did you feel embarrassed?

Prospect 1: Ha-ha-ha ... yeah ... luckily she never saw what happened to me!

Brand: Lol ... happens to the best of us. We fix cars at our workshop. One of our customers drove into a pole watching a sexy babe walk by! Now we got to fix the damages.

Prospect 2: Typical - Men ... they're all the same!

Brand: Human nature, @prospect 2 ☺

Prospect 2: More like hu-men nature!

Brand: Was a lady driver!

Prospect 3: Hehehe no way! Get outa here!

Brand: No problem for us, sir. We got to fix the dent!

Prospect 4: I suppose you pray to God for accidents so you can get business in!

Brand: No Sir, we pray to God for safe roads. There's nothing worse than having to tell a client they won't get their car back the same day!

Prospect 5: Yeah, but surely you give a courtesy vehicle whilst you're fixing it?

Brand: We can only do so once Insurance authorizes it. But, we often go the extra mile. Still, you want quality repairs, we're the best in town!

Prospect 6: My car backfires. What do you suppose the problem is with it?

You get the idea? Social sales is not always about selling, and convincing the prospect there and then to use your services or products. Social sales require conversations! Real down to earth raw in-your-face conversations. Without conversations happening, you will not get far with your brand online.

CEO, MD, COO, FD, GM, whatever O, D, or M you are: your sales team need to be primed for online sales. They have to be ready to jump online and seize the opportunity with customers; to get them to a point where they are willing to talk on the phone, or come in (or if need be, you go to them) whatever it takes to get that lead to a point where they can be converted into money! Engagement, social engagement through online conversations is what makes for lead generation and conversion.

In the above example the initial conversation was simply about the semantics of the post, but it was very quickly and cleverly swung into a conversation bringing the prospects into the core business of the brand. It dealt with PR, public perceptions, stereotyping, and all sorts of things. It in short, turned the brand voice into a human voice, and showed the human element in interacting with the market.

Social sales is all about building those relationships, and getting more and more communications. Not enough brands are doing this, and those that are – like the Coca Cola's and the Samsung's and household brands – these brands essentially coin it!

Again, just to reiterate something here, with the evolving digital marketing landscape, you may need to add additional resource to your marketing team, or otherwise outsource varied functions to social media or digital marketing agencies specializing in engagement to do the job for you. Holding conversations like this is a salesmen hat, and is a full-time job.

In Sun Tzu terms the brand voice and sales force you have performing this function online is your digital army. They need to be trained in people skills; articulate to a high degree; spontaneous, witty, and amped for the task. This is how you earn with social sales.

It is all very well promoting, boosting, and sponsoring your content updates in feeds via Facebook, LinkedIn, Twitter or YouTube; it's very well pumping resource into AdWords and other digital advertising vehicles. However, you need to take action in the form of engagement to get those numbers of followers to a point where they can be converted a step closer to closing them on your product or service offering.

Now, this much said about the sales aspect ... know this: that every engagement is a sales action. You may be thinking, yeah but social media engagement with my brand is more about handling customer complaints and queries and directing them to the right solutions within our company and ... Ok. Stop, right there for a sec. Yes, you are absolutely right! Many brands find themselves in this situation. You know what: you need to handle each and every query that comes your way. You see, people are watching your brand. You screw up, you lose followers and get a bad reputation. Look, you can't please everyone. But at least show you are doing everything in your power as a brand to give that customer service that begs for more.

Also customer service is a way of selling your company. The question is: are you selling your company short in doing so? You answer that one! Promo is the PR way of making your brand known far and wide as possible, and generating excellent perceptions about your company, its staff, its products and services. So, all of these actions sell you, and really, the sky is the limit.

PART 4

FORMATION

The Primary Objective in Applying Strategy

Friends, recap all the above italicized rules of engagement quickly. Absorb it all, short form. Get it down rote. Stick to these rules of war and you will win. We are now about to color everything you've learned so far against this backdrop:

Win the customer – dominate the field

All the rules speak to this core summary for what we are doing here. Your offensive should never ever, under any circumstances, be aimed at your competitor's strengths. Doing so is suicide – it will cost you valuable resource and budget, and I want to see you justify further budget spend to your board. I mean this sarcastically in this sense here.

The best odds to win the war is always and will always be focusing on the customer's needs – your followers (and getting more followers consistently and continuously) - meeting those needs, demands, wants, requests, complaints, compliments, suggestions, whatever, whenever; and bearing in mind your competitor's weaknesses all in one.

It doesn't get easier than that. I'm not even going to break that mouthful down; I've repeated it in the above many times.

This is the secret to master your future survival in the new world. There's a whole new realm of conquest to be entered into. Global businesses are beginning to wake up to the reality that the world as we knew it, is migrating at a phenomenal pace into a world we are yet to know. The C-Suite is traditionally middle-aged upward; and this is not an attack on you dear friends, and colleagues. This is a reality – you've been so busy with high-level stuff; you've lost touch with what is now catching up to you. And you've possibly been naïve and slow to learn; relegating the learning curve for the new generation. Well, what are you going to do when your own existence is now threatened because of technological innovation? Are you going to retire, and Johnny or Matt can take the reigns over? Come on!

There is only one-way for you to stay on top now: that is to learn the new tech, learn the new marketing, and learn the new sales. It's all there still, only its form has changed and it's now on social media and the digital highway. Jump on board. It's not too late, you just need to adapt.

Adapt to the New World [Wide Web] Order

We're no longer in the 80s or 90s; and your mom and dad are busy dying because they're all old now, and only you can survive for you and your kids and loved ones now. You need to master the new world.

It's a digital world.

There are no borders anymore. There's no exchange of cash these days – we now talk about PayPal and Master Card, Visa, and American Express all traded in cyber-dollars. But this is soon drawing to a close. These are slowly being replaced by Bitcoins and other digital currencies that we have to now adapt to. Cash is migrating into cyberspace, and now what? We got the one world currency already baby! The conspiracy theorists are so busy looking at trends to the NWO – new world order - that they cannot see, we're already in the middle of it! This is the New World Order, and you're living in the centre of it! Learn to fight in it.

Sun Tzu is your answer. You have to adapt to it and meet the challenges of the evolving cyber-currency environment. If you are finding it difficult to get to grips with the digital world, put yourself on as many courses as possible to bring you up to speed. Become a Master at it. If you know your way around the digital space, excellent: now what you have to do is become pro and be better than all the rest at it.

I will put you onto an Academy at the end of this book to bring you up to speed. You can learn online or go in person to them, and mix with like-minded people, eat their fancy foods and drink their stuff. It doesn't matter what your thing is, just get in, get the knowledge, and USE this knowledge! Use it like a pro it's your new tools in this new world, if you wish to survive.

What does Sun Tzu say about all of this? Check this out:

The rules of the military are five:

1. Measurement of space
2. Assessment [or] estimation of quantities
3. Calculation of figures
4. Comparison of strengths
5. Victory [or] the chances of success

The [battle] ground gives rise to measurements, measurements give rise to assessments, assessments give rise to calculations, calculations give rise to comparisons, comparisons give rise to victories.

When the victorious get their people to go to battle as if they were directing a massive flood of water into a deep canyon, this is a matter of formation.

Ok, let's unpack this one. The measurement of space is pretty much the initial strategic assessment we did. So, like identifying where we need to fight it out? On social media – which platforms to use, and focus strengths on; where do you have capacity to be? Regarding your website – is it up to scratch to handle what is coming? Emails up and running? Do you have the tools to send mass emails, sms's, all that stuff, you understand? And you can also see where the game is happening by identifying the enemy camps in cyberspace – your competitors.

Your estimation of quantities arises from your SWOT and Competitor's Analyses. You've done a thorough study of what is needed, and what kind of budget will get you to where you ought to be.

Calculation of figures follows on from here – submit your budgets to board, go through all that stuff so you have the clout to man-up and go to war. And here you are also calculating how to benchmark yourself versus your competitors for future evaluation and re-grouping - I would recommend doing this on a quarterly to biannual basis.

To compare strengths, is the key for your survival in this new digital order. So, we're going to turn our attention to analytics, reporting, monitoring and general intel operations in a moment. This is the real news in digital marketing; it's where your substance and survival lays. You see, information, data – big data – is what will give you the edge. The easy part is getting the following, the eyeballs in, if you prefer. A previous stat used to be, how many bodies in the shop. Now things have changed, because essentially your shop is online now. People doodle from the comforts of their homes or the beach now, so why go to your store, your office, your warehouse or whatever, if they can do so online? Get it? So it's now how many eyeballs with money flashing through them like a jackpot machine, can you reach, capture, and convert into sales.

It's really two things that work together – marketing and sales. Digital marketing is the new sales now. And if you hate sales, you had better learn it now or die. As a marketer you are now the salesman; so get with the program.

The last factor or rule in winning business in the new world order digital sphere of things, is victory: pretty much a self-explanatory concept, so I won't go into it for now.

Essentially, what Sun Tzu is saying, is each step of the way to victory is a logical follow-on of the preceding step. You see, with a strategy in place, you've pretty much won the war already! Get that!

With a digital strategy in place you have won the war!

So, clients contact us all the time. They're like we need more followers; we need to make money online; we need to establish ourselves to get more business; we need to migrate our business to the web ... you get it.

People know they need to be doing it online. They know it, but they don't always know *how*! I'm teaching you how, here.

The very first thing we ask the client is: Do you have a strategy? Do you have a digital marketing strategy?

Most of the time they do not – because they don't know how or what they are supposed to be doing. All they know is, there's so much talk of social media and the internet; and they're seeing the population usage stats climbing exponentially on a daily basis; it's simply mind blowing!

Get this – here's some stats to consider the curves on each platform; and these are just a few:

As of this books writing, there is over 3,4 billion Internet users worldwide. That is almost half of the world's population are currently on the Internet! There are also close to 1,1-billion websites on the Internet, with close to 4,2-billion Google searches conducted daily at the time of writing.

Turning to the top social media stats at the time of writing: Facebook clocked in 1,728 billion active users; Facebook in 2004 had 1-million users. By 2008 this grew to 145-million, and by 2012 had jumped to 1-billion! These are absolutely huge strides! Twitter has over 306-million active users.

LinkedIn has 380-million active users as of April 2015. YouTube has over 1-billion users as of 2014. Instagram is growing fast, with 300-million users in 2014. Google Plus had 1,4-billion active users; Pinterest has 72.8-million users in 2015. Skype has over 300-million users, whilst WhatsApp now has more than 1-billion active users in 2016.

You get the picture, right? This is where the active market is. They're increasingly online; they're increasingly engaging you in the digital space. We haven't even jumped on the stats of Periscope, Houseparty, Tinder, Tumblr, or Vine here. The point is you can see very clearly the growth over time. So if you are business-minded I am sure you see the value of being online. Being online exposes you to the volumes of users you see in the above table!

You may have had a local business exposed to your city and surrounding suburbs, and by word of mouth maybe scored some sales outside of town, whatever. Now you can have the same business online, exposed to a global community, which even if you zap 0.5% of it to buy, you can retire comfortably forever.

Get it? You're just no longer needing to place so many newspaper ads, and having people standing on street corners or in shopping malls handing out costly flyers that mostly end up in the bin in any event. Or paying some premium for the local post office to kindly place your flyers in each post box. You also don't have to pay for expensive TV Ads or Radio Ads anymore and wait for the station to find you a slot. Now you simply upload to YouTube, or whichever of these networks and maybe pay a tiny premium compared to before to have your ad seen in the networks. Or you send out some mailer to your database, or update your newsletter, whatever – so many more ways to skin a cat today.

So, what's your strategy to win the war for business on the Internet? That's the first question I always ask a customer or client. And we routinely and standardly apply these principles >> Conduct a Strategic Assessment of what you got and what is needed >> Conduct a SWOT and Competitors Analysis to know what you're up against and where you can gain market share >> throw resource at preparing for war >> go to war!

Going to war is simply this >> conducting simultaneous content marketing campaigns whilst targeting your profiled customers.

What you waiting for? Execute what you planned, because your strategic plan is in place now, and you will win!

All you have to do now is simply evaluate your actions as you implement and execute each step of the way. And this is done through the use of analytics, reports, and vigilant monitoring of the digital environment.

To evolve with the times, you need to constantly receive new knowledge and be trained on new, fresh ways of doing things. So, you need stay well informed – both about your competitors and customers; and also about the battlefields you select to fight in.

Facebook, especially, is known to be a highly evolving medium. The folks at Facebook are always adapting and innovating upon the platform, to enhance their delivery of the ad environment; or to accommodate new apps released into the foray; or with new things they add in, new services for users and so forth. As a result, their algorithms change, and this changes the very nature of your reach and engagement – so these kinds of factors need to be monitored. These are the climate changes on the battlefield that determine how and when you fight for customers.

PART 5

INTELLIGENCE

Routine Reporting

For this section, I refer to Sun Tzu's Art of War chapters on Adaptation, Manoeuvering Armies and The Use of Spies. The only way a General is able to manoeuvre with skill, is through foresight. In battle the General has available on hand several sources of information through a network of spies. He also has reports from the troops on the battlefield in order to correlate, corroborate and validify information. In this regard Sun Tzu advises the use of spies. Now, obviously we're not going to take this literally here, for espionage, industrial espionage, cyber-espionage are very real commodities in the information industry, but probably not for your business. In fact, these espionage tactics only really impede upon your business through hackers, cyber-snoopers, and the things they use to access info on you.

Here, Sun Tzu evidences the point that as a strategist, you need intelligence, information from another source to ascertain your progress, as well as with which to execute your next strategic and tactical moves.

> A major military operation is a severe drain on the nation, and may be kept up for years in the struggle for one day's victory. So to fail to know the conditions of opponents because of reluctance to give rewards for intelligence is extremely inhumane, uncharacteristic of a true military leader, uncharacteristic of an assistant of the government, uncharacteristic of a victorious chief. So what

> enables an intelligent government and a wise military leadership to overcome others and achieve extraordinary accomplishments is foreknowledge.
>
> Foreknowledge cannot be gotten from ghosts and spirits, cannot be had by analogy, cannot be found out by calculation. It must be obtained from people, people who know the conditions of the enemy.

Who gave you the initial foreknowledge of your competitors? Whoever compiled your competitors' analysis, right? Something interesting here, remember all the calculations involved in that foreknowledge? Yet here Sun Tzu says it doesn't stem from calculations, but from people? He is 100% on the mark. Why? As much as what war is a calculation of strengths and weaknesses, opportunities and threats, it is an art. Judgement calls are needed to embark on various courses of action. Your calculations need to be interpreted into whatever is deemed vital for an operation. So, at the end of the day, you are going to collect data, electronic data, with all kinds of fancy descriptors and *someone* needs to interpret these metrics (quantitative indicators of data) and make sense of what is going on.

Who?

There is none better than the social media team working on your account. And none better than the manager, supervisor, or team leader running your marketing show. Sun Tzu is well aware that you may be fighting these battles for many years still to come. You see, even once you have risen to greatness and become that F500 – your fight will then change into maintaining and retaining your dominance and improving on it. There will be other competitors who will eventually embark on the course of action you are now on; your competitors may even cotton on and execute similar strategies. So, you need a very loyal team on your side that will maintain course and direction, and inculcate themselves into the fabric of the digital battlefield.

You MUST have them develop a system of regular reporting. My recommendation is weekly following and engagement reports.

These can be committed to a daily basis whenever you embark on blitz campaigns such as advertising and campaigns through paid for or rather boosted and sponsored posts. I further recommend a monthly report based on your website and social media analytics.

You can develop your own framework for what kinds of data to include. I will give you a couple of vital things you should be including in your reporting, as well as some ways the data can be interpreted. Remember the key concept to grasp here, is to treat these indicators as statistics, because that is essentially what they are. To derive good interpretations of these statistics you will need to naturally view these over a period of time. My advice is to view these stats over a period of 3-6 months.

Website Analytics

I recommend the use of Google Analytics, which is excellently structured, and accessible. The analytics are essentially free of charge from Google, as long as you have a Gmail account, configured to your website. I'm not going to explain how to configure it or get the plug-in here, and so forth – please do get your Webmaster or web developer to ensure this is set-up for you. I'm more concerned here with what kind of analytics are available, how to use them, interpret them and make meaningful interpretations from the data that arises.

The first thing you will need to do when accessing your Analytics – which is done via google.com/analytics – and then signing into your gmail account to which it is configured, is to set the date range you wish to inspect. I usually just set it for the month, or the last 90-days.

By default, the platform is set to first provide you with an Audience Overview. This is where you will find a graph and pie chart with several smaller graphs. Generally, this provides an excellent website performance overview for the period in question; and you can also see to click on the time tabs to get a better perspective of things by the hour, day, week, or month.

These analytics are fairly self-explanatory – sessions are basically how many times your website has been hit by followers. This is a sum of new (or unique) visitors and repeat visitors, as identified electronically by the IP address from which they hail. The overview is further broken down into the number of users of the website, and how many page views accumulated though their visits. Good indicators for monitoring engagement, especially if your site has several things on offer – such as a fashion, or retail site. You can also view the average number of pages viewed per session, and how long people spend on your site.

Coming to the bounce rate – this is of vital importance to your general performance. There are a number of things you can do to tweak performance, and this is also an important analytic to monitor to see that people are engaging with you online through your website. Bounce rate is the percentage of single page visits, wherein the visitor left your site without clicking further than the page they landed on. The higher this % - the worse the state of affairs, and you cannot expect to land much business or enjoy much lead generation with a high bounce rate. You need at least 26% and downwards – the closer to 0% in bounce rate, the better it is for your business! Therefore, if you have a high bounce rate, you need to ask why are people not clicking any further.

A number of factors could be responsible for this: the page takes long to load; the content is boring and people have already seen your stuff before; your site is maybe not optimized for mobile, so takes extra-long to load ... something. You need to find the why and then remedy that fast!

Scrolling down below the overview panel is the demographics of visitors to your site. You can use this to match your target customer whom we profiled above. More or less anyway. Very important to track your conversions, a general conversion overview is found by clicking on the View Full Report link to the bottom right of the demographics panel. You will get a new page that details per country, where the sessions were logged, how your website performed on each segment and how your conversion rate is doing. Again, I'm not going to immerse you in the technical details and intricacies of each metric here, simply just an overview. To fine tune your conversions, goals, completions and what the conversion value is – this will tell your board what your ROI is on marketing spend – you will have to patiently sift through the program or input sequence on the conversion metrics to be able to receive quantifiable results from this particular statistic.

You can also click on the City, Continent, or Sub-content links for a separate breakdown to help you gain insight into exactly where the interest has arisen in the world. It was quite an interesting exercise with a client once serviced, who believed her target resided in Poland and Scandinavian countries. The ads were consequently targeted to those regions, but with very little results (traffic to the website as well as conversions). After analyzing a few months of this data, we realized the initial traffic was coming primarily from France and Russia, Kazakhstan and the Ukraine. We immediately launched new ad campaigns targeted at those countries, and were ecstatic when results picked up far in excess of what we had anticipated.

That much said about conversions and tracking these conversions here, you will also need to get into the whole Google Adspend network through AdWords.

You will further find a side bar on the left-panel of your dashboard that contains four primary analytics: audience, acquisition, behaviour and conversions. These analytics give specific finetuned metrics pertinent to those segments. Each of these analytics has their own overview panels, similar to the Audience overview we have just perused.

Within the Acquisition analytic you will find your AdWords and can analyze exactly where the traffic has been referred to your website from. It is within this panel, and systematically going through each drop-down to impute values into monitoring your goal creation on the different analytics you wish to track. You will find there is a tab for social, where you can create social goals to monitor how your ads on social media perform when referrals come to your site. Another excellent indicator for ROI based on your marketing budget.

If you're not getting ROI, then you're doing something wrong, and this will be your first port of call to go investigate what's happening in your networks and on your site to see why they're not converting beyond a lead.

Network Referrals are useful to show how much traffic indeed is routed from your social media sites to your website, if any. I say if any, because you may find no data despite having click-through's on your LinkedIn Posts for example. This would then indicate a bounced customer – maybe something wrong with the link itself, or what you thought was a click through was in fact just a click on the image to see it better on social media. You would have to check this out to understand it better, and your findings will enable you to prevent a missed opportunity in future.

The behaviour analytic in the side panel when clicked on will give you the behaviour overview panel, again self-explanatory. This analytic panel is especially helpful in determining why your bounce rate is not what it should be, especially if you suspect the page is loading too slow. This analytic panel will reveal all of these finer things to you. Google Analytics in fact has a unique Speed Suggestions function located in this panel, whereby you can click on the link given and you will be directed to a new page, called Page Speed Insights. You can instruct the Google App to explore your website both on mobile and desktop to suggest how to improve matters. It takes a few minutes, and you will be given a list of issues to remedy, with links on how to do so.

This will for sure fix your bounce rate and page speed settings, giving no excuse as to why customers cannot get to you, or stay on your page. You may need to work with your web developer on this, to ensure technical soundness of the actions to be performed as many times the actions recommended involve making adjustments within HTML or CSS and JavaScript on your web pages. As with Sun Tzu if you're not trained on a particular weapon, simply don't use it! Same principle applies in this instant.

Lastly, the Conversions Analytic panel at the bottom of your side bar gives you access to a whole world of really juicy data, especially when running an ecommerce site, that is one with a shopping cart facility. Again, you will need to patiently configure these sections with the right data in order for the analytics to be accurate and to serve you with information that is found. This analytic panel will give you key data concerning your products (as in stock control over the internet to a certain extent), sales performance, transactions, timing of transactions, and so forth.

You will have to play around with these analytics to see what would best work for you and your business. After some time, you will find which metric hold meaning for you, and then focus on those. I for one generally just use the Audience Overview and Network Referral panels, together with the Conversions Panel when there is ad spend involved from the website point of view.

I think you would agree with me that Google Analytics is an extremely comprehensive platform. It is highly customizable too, and generally a free service within the Google package. Well, I say that tongue in cheek because you end up paying for it through AdWords and other Google products in any event. Given this, and the highly technical nature of all these fancy stats, you might want to consider either employing a Digital Analyst onto your team, whose primary responsibility will compile Intel on your behalf and make succinct recommendations on the various actions noted during the marketing process. Having your finger on the pulse with such a resource can only serve you well.

Alternatively, you may wish to train your marketing staff through Google's Analytics Academy, in order to achieve the GAIQ qualification – the Google Analytics Individual Qualification, where such people can practice as analysts. These are what Sun Tzu would label your "spies" because essentially these people will provide you with an invaluable product to keep your marketing and digital marketing strategy on track. Bear in mind that the program is essentially free of charge, there's no fee for this; however, like I said nothing is ever for free – you need to be a Google Partner for this, which means you need to have done 6-months of advertising through Google AdWords prior to being awarded the title "partner". A small price to pay if you're really serious about making money online. It is up to you where you want to go with all of this, and naturally depends on your budget. For F500's this is really a pee in the ocean! Excellent Intel is the only way to get you to the top and dominate your industry.

I can almost bet: your competitors are not even doing this yet.

Social Media Analytics

Each of the Big 3 social media platforms has their own internal analytics you can access. I personally find these quite useful and no need to subscribe to further analytic providers who will give me the same results. That is a matter of preference though. You do get providers who can give you all your analytics from one domain, instead of having to login to each platform for individual reports.

Facebook

Go to your Facebook Page – unfortunately you can't access personal page analytics, as this is more for companies or business. I'm sure in future Facebook will be gracious and afford everyone the democratic privilege of exploring his or her personal stats! But ok, never mind, for now, we make use of the available resources.

To access these analytics, you will find an "Insights" Tab next to your notifications. Click that and we'll take a quick trip through the platform from there.

This is a highly useful analytic platform and also opens in an overview panel. Data in the first 3 graphs shows your activity over the past week. This concerns page likes, reach and engagement over the past week. Scrolling down you have your 5 most recent posts with several post performance indicators.

Scrolling down to the last section on this Overview Panel is something you really want to take note of, as this short circuits your analysis of how your competitors are doing under Pages to Watch. In this panel, you can add up to 10 competitors' pages you would like to keep track of on Facebook. It gives an awesome run down of their digital market share and engagement. This is excellent to determine on a weekly basis what is happening; and at a glance in keeping cognizant of the figures you can see when a competitor is running a campaign, or merely marking time. This is very useful to spot the opportunity and weaknesses with. Also by just hovering your mouse over the bar stat of the particular measurement, you will get a pop-up with exact figures.

The only drawback with this panel is you HAVE TO keep a weekly stat count of your competitors, because there's no historical record or exportable csv or spreadsheet of this particular data. So, until Facebook amend this in their frequent changes, you just have to get into a regular habit of monitoring. Assign someone in your team the specific task of doing so, and capture your data in your own spreadsheet format for reference as needed. You can also graph this for a quick overview on your end.

You will notice in the top right hand area of Facebook Insights, is an export tab. This is where you can export historical analytics dating back to the last 500 posts at a time. You can choose to export your page, post or video data in either xls or csv format, whichever you prefer. I personally re-edit the data once exported and highlight the metrics I am interested in for quick reference. You will also find when it comes to reach and impressions, Facebook very considerately breaks down these figures into daily, weekly and 28 day scores. What I do is insert a couple of lines under the headings in each export, and then calculate the SUM (3: whatever) in the xls formula bar, and drag the formula across the spreadsheet so I can get the totals for the months' reach or impressions, which incidentally sometimes needs to accommodate for 30 or 31 days. Use your discretion here. The totals are really all you are interested in. Just also be mindful that some of the SUM totals are irrelevant, as in Page Likes – which Facebook logs on a daily-accumulative basis and not as a daily figure beginning at zero.

All I really use the export files for is for the reach and impressions, and sometimes, what I do is sort the rows so that I have posts descending for the time period per post reach and impressions down to the least. That way I can see what successful actions I had with those posts that did well: maybe it was the timing, or the content (or these were boosted), and then I can also see where I screwed up and never achieved good rates for reach and impressions.

Next to the Overview tab are the Likes, Reach, Visits, Posts, Videos and People tabs. Each of these is self-explanatory. When you go into these respective analytic panels, you will find a clear distinction between Organic and Paid posts. Also when you hover your mouse over any part of the graphs in these analytic panels, pop-ups will give you more precise data for those particular spots on the graphs.

Click on the Posts Tab. This is golden data when you understand how it works. Only two panels appear on this analytics page: the first shows when people are online. The second details the summaries of your posts or updates done. All the posts you publish can be analyzed in terms of their reach and engagement. This section also shows you whether you boosted the post or not. Incidentally you can also see the summary of your campaign or boosted post here, as well as how much you have remaining if the campaign has not yet been exhausted. So, in this way you can easily keep tabs on what you're doing. Note you can also view organic and paid reach by clicking the arrow button next to the Title Row at the top of this panel, as can be done for specific data on "Post Clicks" and so forth. Remember to click on the "See More" link below each panel to allow you access to data further back in your feed.

Scrolling to the top, we get to where you find the sweet spots to post things and to reach your audience. This is when you surprise your enemies. In the middle is a huge grey blob on a graph. This shows the average times when users are online; and by gauging the vertical rise of the graph, you can see how many users are online at any given time of the day. Simply hover your mouse there to get an idea of what I am saying here. The grey blob is representative of the trend of when your followers are online – and does not necessarily represent exactness, so rather just use it as a guideline, not a definitive.

Where you can become much more exacting is in the hover blocks above the graph. Each represents a day of the week, and the analytics are updated weekly. So, the more regular you are online, posting and engaging through Facebook, the more people will be in your networks, and obviously the more engagement you can expect the more known you make yourself. Hover your mouse over any particular day, and you will see a black line mark itself over the graph. This line is the exactitude for that particular day, and may in places be higher than the norm, or under par. If you find in a particular week it has been under par, you will need to go and check on that day what happened. It may have been you failed to post, or you never got good engagement, or you've lost followers, or something. Only you will be able to see, so you will need to be in the know at all times. This is extremely pertinent for your social media manager or community manager, whoever is assigned to lead your troops onto the daily battlefield. Also vital for you as the general and strategist reading this book to understand: that way no bullshit, and you get to stay in charge.

Where the graph line peaks, is where you want to post. This is where you will receive the best organic growth; and more importantly when you want to boost a post, as more people are online then. You can also see, when it is a quiet day, and when it is really hectic. Unfortunately, Facebook at this stage only posts this data pertinent to your time zone per your IP. Hopefully in future Facebook will enable time zone metrification so you can better target sweet spots for posts to be seen in different parts of the world.

By clicking on the Post Types tab in this analytic panel, you will be given a summary of the types of posts you are using in your content mix – usually these are just photos, links and videos. And you will get the total reach and engagement for these kinds of posts. I don't pay too much attention to this analytic simply because your content mix demands just that – a mix of different types of content posts. If you don't have a mix, your page will become monotonous and repetitive, and detract from things being social. Feel free to post videos – at the present time as this book is being written, Facebook awards better EdgeRank to video posts than to photos and links. That is also because Facebook wants you to boost more photos. As an IPO they have to make their money, right?

If you click on the next tab in this panel, "Top Posts from Pages You Watch" you will be given the list of your competitors from the Overview Panel, with their top performing posts for the week. This is also extremely useful data as it tells you in a flash what your competitors are doing. Top posts attract top engagement. Engagement attracts loyalty and conversion opportunities. So, you want to stay in the loop and plan counter-attacks accordingly.

The last tab in the Facebook Insights page is "People". Here you get the demographics of those in your community in terms of gender, country, city and language. This may or may not correspond to the demographics you have from your website traffic. Remember each social media platform is also unique in its demographics; but you nevertheless get a good idea here whether you are on track with your targeted profiled customer, or not. These analytics are also hierarchically composed, meaning you can easily see where most of your fans are located in each segment.

The first tab on the People Analytics panel is Your Fans. These are just that: all the fans who have liked your page. They do not necessarily need to be active on your page. The second tab is People Reached, and this is the demographics of the people reached in your Facebook network over the past 28 days. Facebook calculates 28-day cycles, as these are equal increments of a 13-month year, rather than a day or two extra each month for a 12-month year.

The last tab here is "People Engaged" and this is pretty much those who engaged with your brand over the past month. This is what you want to keep tabs on, because you will quickly see how close to your profiled customer you are. If you are off the mark, the only thing you can do is to engage in really targeted advertising, where you can define your audience better. My suggestion would be to blitz your ad campaign with higher than usual revenues – so instead of spending say $350 per month, spend $500 for this month to get the audience in. You can always reach them organically to compensate for reduced ad spend due to budget constraints in the following month.

The demographics are really fantastic, because they tell you whom your content needs to speak to. If you have mostly men in the 25-34 bracket and who are located in Germany who engage with your brand; then you need to speak more to them with suitable content and messages tailored for them. Research that demographic niche more in depth if needed, and develop suitable content therein. However, if this is off the mark, then you need to cut the kind of content you are running – because it is clearly attracting the wrong crowd; and then remodel, and repurpose the content to speak to the demographic you really want. And remember, always when rectifying this state of affairs, increase your ad spend and generate targeted ad spends for that month, to pull followers into the niche demographic that aligns better with that of your profiled customer.

Always speak to your target audience. This is your profiled customer from the beginning of this book. Targeting anybody outside of this is as good as shooting the innocents in war. Waste of time, and can only land you in trouble. Imagine all that wasted budget!

Twitter

To access your Twitter Analytics, I am assuming you have already configured it to your Twitter account. Unlike Facebook, you can configure it for any account provided you have the handle and login details – analytics.twitter.com – or if already done, simply login to your account, click on your profile icon next to the settings tab and navigate down to analytics. The analytic platform will open in a new tab.

Steer yourself there and then we talk further.

The home page in your Twitter Analytics shows a brief 28-day summary of your performance. Below that are pockets of summaries for each month going backwards on your profile. Here you will find your top tweet, top mention, top follower and top media tweet (something you retweeted). You can also click on the View Tweet Activity tab in each summary to obtain more specific summary analytics of the particular Tweet – such as Favorites, Clicks, Engagements and Impressions.

The mini-summary graphs also show you whether you're up or down from the previous month. And you will therefore know from the outset to take action.

Click on the "Tweets" Tab next to the home button on the top navigation panel. A new Tweet Activity page will open. You will immediately see an impressions graph, where you can hover over it for precise stats for that day of the month- in terms of Number of Tweets done that day and Total Impressions generated for those Tweets too. You can also select your date range from the "Last 28 Days" tab for customized data. And of course you can export this data in csv format.

First select your date range before exporting data, otherwise you will only export data for the past 28-days. As with Facebook exported data, I also delete the columns and rows unnecessary to my purposes; and insert a few blank rows at the top in order to calculate the totals for the data under consideration. All I usually use from this information is the Engagements column, and so that by re-ordering the data for top to smallest performing tweets in terms of impressions, I can see at a glance how the content performed for the month. The rest of the data is usually available as you see on this page.

By scrolling down you will find in the right hand column the Engagement Rate, Link Clicks, Retweets, Favorites and Replies. The total figure is easily spotted as well as a hover graph where placement of your mouse will show the specific analytic on a given day. You will also see in the Tweet summary list to the left, you can check on the performance of each tweet on any given day of the month going backwards. The impression graph also shows the total volume of impressions. If you want a more exact figure, simply hover over each bar on the graph and add the figures up. The summary figure is rounded off, usually.

The Twitter Analytics are pretty straightforward. You will also see the promoted Tweets segments of the analytics are similar to those pulled up in Facebook for boosted posts: the idea is conveyed along the same principle – that of paid reach versus organic.

When you click on the Followers Tab, you will receive what I believe is far better demographic indicators than those found on Facebook. On Twitter you are able to see what your followers' interests are, as well as the consumer buying styles, net worth, marital status, education and level of home ownership. I believe this is a far superior analytic platform than Facebook's because it speaks more to business that Facebook Analytics. I wish Facebook would implement similar analytics on its platform as these make better business sense.

With Twitter demographic indicators you can really streamline your content. You see – Oh 60% of my audience prefer comedy and finance news: that tells me as a marketing strategist the kind of content to prepare: humorous and with a financial newsy bearing. That will get my audience more engaged and favouriting more stuff to share to their networks. Even down to the wireless carrier can be analyzed, so I know maybe to include some RT's from the dominant wireless carriers per the demographic data. The followers will think, OMG – this brand is good! They even have what I use! You get the picture?

Under the Overview Tab on this panel, you will see your Following Graph, hover over it for a particular count on any day of the month. You can also see where spikes in your growth path are. So, you will want to trace whatever successful actions were done on the days you had bursts of growth, and make this a repetitive action.

Click the demographics tab for specific data relating to language and country. These are also monetized indicators, to help you with predictive targeting patterns. Click on the Lifestyle tab and you will also be able to see more pertinent information, classing even the TV genres your followers prefer. See, all this data helps with engagement planning for your content. If I know last night Seinfeld was aired, and this data shows my followers prefer that kind of genre, I can tweet a couple of tweets first thing in the morning or throughout the day, something tailored about last night's Seinfeld show. I am bound to receive better engagement, not to mention RT's and Favs! Try it out, I tell you it works.

Click on Consumer Behaviour and you will find more data about the consumer patterns in your network. Unfortunately, these demographics are more correct for US markets at the time of writing. However, these will migrate globally in due course, and therefore best to keep a good eye on these patterns.

I will leave you to have fun with this most brilliant analytic platform in future. Not going through all the details, simply an overview of what is offered here. The point to be emphasized is this is yet another analytic platform to streamline your marketing efforts. As a strategist you will monitor the info gleaned from these analytics.

And you will use it through the insights you draw to steer and guide your marketing team on the ground to use tactical prowess in gaining followers, converting them into sales leads, and in combatting your competitors on all fronts so that you can dominate the digital space.

LinkedIn

Linked has two main analytic sources. The one is for your published posts, and personal stats. The other source concerns your company page performance analytics. To get you to your post views, simply click on your profile drop-down tab and click on "Your Updates" option. This will take you to where your recent activity is found – published posts, and drafts. Click on the "Published Posts" tab and then find the Stats button right beside the Publish a Post button. Click that and you'll be taken to a net summary that is customizable for what you want to examine. You can also access these stats by simply going to the drop-down on your profile and selecting the Who's Viewed your Profile link. We'll go through this in a second.

To get to your company page performance, simply navigate to the page and then you will see the Home, Analytics, and Notifications tabs. Click on Analytics, and you are in.

The first analytic panel you see is your updates. You can scroll through them and click the "See More" link to go as far back as you like. In this panel you will see all your sponsored posts, impressions, clicks, interactions, followers acquired as a result, and engagement rates. A quick overview of your updates will pinpoint where you did best.

The next analytic panel is your reach and engagement. You have the option to click the time drop-down and select how you wish to view this, and over what time frame. This is excellent for month end reporting. When you hover your mouse on the graph lines you also see the values for that particular day. LinkedIn's drawback is in order to reach the macro-picture you will have to manually add up each day's score in the time frame you selected. The graphs also helpfully differentiate between paid and organic values. The great thing is that you are able at an eye glance to see where you did well, and particularly on which dates, and can trace these back to the specific posts to determine what the successful actions were. As a corollary, you can work out how best to enhance those areas you see as having been poor in performance, in future.

LinkedIn does have a link there to give you some tips on what to do to improve engagement on the platform. Be wise enough to study this, as these are proven ways of achieving success when it comes to engagement.

Next up is your followers and follower demographics. There is a drop-down besides the default "seniority" title to be able to select demographics by industry, company size, function and employee. A brief summary is given as to your performance in relation to other competitors the platform has identified. Unfortunately, these may not necessarily be the competitors you wish to monitor, and at this stage there is no way of defining these on the LinkedIn Platform. I am sure in due course as the platform rolls out more developments; this will be addressed and made possible.

Scrolling further down you will find Visitor Analytics. Once again you can select your date range as required, and determine the volume of unique visitors and page views. Finally, the visitor demographics are analyzed and also with the drop-down for more targeted information in terms of seniority, industry, company size and function.

The only analytics available for personal profile pages are those related to your published posts and profile. Let's take a quick look. Click the link on your home page: "Who's Viewed your Profile". The stats you find are calculated over the past 90 days. Until you are able to export this data, you will have to remain ever so vigilant on the platform to reproduce the data off-platform for your own analytic purposes. Remember where I suggested you employ an Analyst for this. Hell of a lot of work to constantly and consistently monitor such data.

Here you can see how many profile views you had in relation to actions done. Again, you will soon understand what is working and what is not. These analytics are especially useful for the brand ambassadors at the forefront of your brand. Your C-Suite probably being the persons whose LinkedIn Profiles should be inspected for this analytic data. However, you will first need their buy-in and consent with logins to monitor them. If not, they will have to somehow pull reports so you can keep track and advise on what to do for them to steer themselves in the right direction in unison with your brand.

The next tab to the right of Profile Views shows where your viewers work and live; that is to say which company. The third tab will show you what work your viewers do, and which industry they are in. You can also hover over segments of the pie chart here to garner further data.

If you scroll down beneath this analytic panel, you will find some recommendations that LinkedIn coughs up for you to improve your performance. You don't have to do any of these. But the platform does seem to know what is best to do, so, use your discretion here. I can tell you the key to growth on LinkedIn as with any digital marketing lies in the power of your blog. LinkedIn has its own blog in the form of published posts, which go straight onto the category tags you select and these align with various things on LinkedIn Pulse – which is the newspaper, the reader on the platform that everyone has access to. So, the more you publish, the more you get seen, and people follow you and connect with you, and the rest is history. You can very soon become a huge influencer in your particular field. Anyway, back to the analytics.

When you click on the "Who Viewed Your Posts" tab, you will see your published posts running from left to right. Also a graph that shows the performance of each post. Again select the time range you need, and the following indicators will be populated – Views, Likes, Comments, Shares. Scrolling further south, you get to the demographic indicators of your viewers, by industry, job title, location and traffic source. You will see how people have come to you. So, if you post an update with the link to your article on any of the social media platforms, your viewers will be referenced from whence they came. OMG I just used Victorian English! Lol.

And of course you will even see who is responding to your post. So, LinkedIn does something the other social media platforms do not do: it shows you who your leads really are by name! If you are vigilant enough, you will actually go on the persons' profile, connect with them if they are not yet connected to you, and determine what they could be after. You can in other words prequalify a lead simply by checking out their profile. In which case, inbox them, get them on the phone do whatever it takes to close them on something!

You can then click on the last tab in this analytic panel, how you rank for profile views, and LinkedIn will show you just where you fit in, and if you are up or down from last month. Now, depending on what you wish to achieve with this platform, you will want to adopt a strategy to get you into the top 5% amongst professionals similar to you, globally, and also into the top 5% of all your connections. When you can get this right, you're a fucking legend!

The nice thing about LinkedIn's analytic methodology is it shows real people against whom to benchmark yourself. So, in this particular tab, you will see the top 10 most viewed connections in your network – your competitors! And in case you did not know they were; now you do! You can then jump to where you fit in and scroll up or down to see who the contenders are in your immediate league. Again, like I say, blog more, publish more posts, become the thought leader; be the guru - and you will rocket into the top 10 in no time at all.

If you click the alternate tab, "Professionals Like You", you will see firstly you need to be a premium member here to access this stat. When you can access it, you will quickly learn how you rank in this circle of things too. An even more competitive league than your connections, because your connections quite frankly are located in many walks of life. Whereas professionals like you – are all pretty much in the same industry.

As of this writing, LinkedIn was updating its analytics and also its layout; so some of the things may appear in new places soon. I will be sure to publish a blog on the revisions, to keep you in the loop.

Are your eye's wide open yet to how analytic data can be used to streamline your strategic planning and daily, weekly, monthly – hourly if need be handling of marketing in the digital space? This is really a very interesting part of marketing, and very niche to say the least. It's not everybody's cup of tea, but you simply have to get the hang of it to survive in a very competitive world. Your competitor's in all likelihood have not even been exposed to this kind of data yet, so the earlier you get the hang of it, the better you will do, and find yourself rising to the top and dominating your market.

Analytics for other social media platforms

This can be exhaustive to go through in one book, and perhaps another book, simply dedicated to analytics will be appropriate. Suffice it to say, all you are really interested in by analytics is the use these have to manoeuvre you into a dominant position (or as academics refer to a position of competitive advantage).

I concern myself with the number of followers, only because of the reach this gives, or rather can give. I'm also concerned about the engagement – because this generates leads. Naturally I am concerned about reach – how many people can my brand be exposed to? How many opportunities will this mean for me to make myself known and able to pull them in for a sale.

YouTube, Vimeo ... your video channels are interesting when it comes to analytics, because the substantive stats are not so much in the following, the likes, engagement or such. You're after views here. Psy's Gangnam Style got overnight success with more than 1-billion views! And this sure translated through sales of his hit. Check out all the rock stars from Rihanna, Lady Gaga and Nikki Minaj who follow suite with high volumes of views. That's pretty much the major analytic their marketers worry about. (They don't worry, because they're simply cutting it the minute they hit over a million views anyway ... you get the point!)

Remaining with the video-based medium, Houseparty, Periscope and Vine have similar analytic platforms. Periscope has its own dashboard, which is absolutely fabulous, with really vital and key data. What is interesting is Periscope's high degree of integration with Twitter; through its hearts and shared broadcasts, and replay views. Very key indicators of how a broadcaster is doing, and as shown above, using your discretion and intuition to read between the lines, between the figures to reach valid conclusions on courses of action to pursue.

I have left a list at the end of this book of suitable analytic platforms you may access to give you the edge on the most popular platforms in the social media space.

CONCLUSION

Whilst this book has only dealt with particular aspects of digital strategy, centered on the compilation of competitor's analyses, customer profiling and reporting methodologies; it should be remembered that there are many more digital marketing and sales strategies to which Sun Tzu can be applied. What an exciting application of Sun Tzu's Art of War to the Digital Age this book has been though. I truly trust you have gained great wisdom and insights as have been elucidated in this text.

To sum up the main ideas of applying digital strategy to the business context you need to be aware that there is no one size fits all strategy. This book highlights the principles and acts as a guideline for what you can and should be doing to make your business, your brand a market leader, and a dominant force to be reckoned with. The war is not an aggressive one once sufficient market domination has been achieved, because then you will simply influence the outcomes. However, you need to apply aggressive marketing tactics to position yourself as the dominant player in your field or industry.

The digital world never sleeps. You are connected 24/7/365. Your market is global, unless you choose to narrow it down to regional or local relevance.

Any strategic application should always begin with an honest and ethical assessment of where you are at, and where your competitors and prospects are. Competitors are not the prize in war. However, they also are looking for what you want: followers or prospective customers, and you want them to buy your stuff. If you don't have what it takes to convert that follower into a sale in due course, they will surely buy from your competitor.

The importance of knowing who your competitors are is not to compete against them as may traditionally be thought. Instead, you are merely making yourself aware of what they are doing to win market share and dominance themselves. You just need to be better, and sharper so you can offer prospects a better product or service.

Your strategic assessment will seek to answer five things: how much influence do you have in the market place? What challenges do you face to assert greater influence than what you currently are? What and who exactly is your market? What is your marketing team doing to gain more share out there, and to capture meaningful share that translates into cash in the bank? How focused and disciplined is your marketing effort to ensure wads of cash in the bank?

Next you will compile a comprehensive profile of your typical customer. You will also compile a SWOT analysis both of your top competitors and yourself. We have explored the steps to understanding in-depth how competitors are winning market share, as well as yourself. You can determine what is working or not. To this end from a digital perspective, you will need to systematically examine how competitors are performing through their websites, and their social media. You will also need to examine their content marketing strategies, to see what you ought to be doing to gain the upper hand.

The thing about business today is the need to occupy and be extremely active in the digital space. It is a very busy sphere of activity requiring a re-purposing of traditional marketing methods.

The move is flowing away from traditional media such as newspapers and magazines, and is migrating rapidly onto digital platforms where the onus is now on controlling the ad-space through your own pages. You are now responsible for your own market share.

Previously you could simply advertise through a newspaper, with a known average daily readership of x-million. From there you could more or less gauge that for the frequency of your ad campaigns you could expect y-feet in the shop and z-closes of sales. Today you don't have a readership of x-million. Newspaper ads do not necessarily work the same for you as before as they have dwindling readerships, and even those readership communities are migrating online. What you do have is your *own network*, your own readership if you like. If you want to access a more global audience, you can; in fact, you can now do something the newspaper could not: you can target your typical audience – and for way less than it previously cost placing an ad in the paper.

Given this power you now have at your fingertips; your marketing efforts are all in your own control. In Sun Tzu's terminology you can now Do Battle. Previously the battle was pretty much fought for you by the print media and other mass media vehicles. You hardly did any *active* marketing, other than the design and layout of your ad. With digital media, it's gotten a lot more sophisticated, and you now need the employ of a graphic designer, a content marketer, a curator, a community manager, a customer representative, a this and a that. You need a new digital sales and marketing force who are trained to follow up on prospects and engage them to get your offering into their hands. Developing and adopting the right policy to your active marketing, combined with an application of the rules of engagement in the market place, will only benefit you and set you up for success.

Business has migrated from bodies in the shop, to eyes in your online store. How to maximize your conversions of online prospects was examined through the derivation of suitable market intelligence from big data sources found on relevant freely available analytic platforms. The war, so to speak, is simply a war for online market share. This is best evidenced in expanding networks and capturing followers. At its ultimate it is seen in the conversion of these digital spoils of the war into sales. Intel you can now access makes this even more possible than before.

My wish in your application of this book, is that you dominate and influence your industry online and in business. The strategic principles of Sun Tzu show you how to win customers and how to earn with social sales.

SOURCES

Michaelson, G.A. and Michaelson, S. 2011, *The Complete Sun Tzu for Business Success: use the classic rules of the Art of War to win the battle for customers and conquer the competition*. Adams Media: Massachusetts, USA.

Cleary, T (translator). 1991, *The Art of War: Sun Tzu* (Pocket Classics). Shambala: Massachusetts, USA.

Internet Usage Statistics
http://www.internetlivestats.com

Social Media Statistics
http://expandedramblings.com/index.php/resource-how-many-people-use-the-top-social-media/

RECOMMENDED ANALYTIC PLATFORMS

These are the most popular local analytics service providers:

    www.sproutsocial.com
    www.hubspot.com
    www.simplymeasured.com

You may also want to look at integrating these platforms into whatever CRM software you may be using to manage your marketing team. Here are a few excellent CRM hosts:

    www.ambition.com
    www.infusion.com
    www.salesforce.com

Salesforce developed an excellent CRM solution for use across several facets of your online management, including your sales, marketing and production teams. From a strategic POV you are also able to monitor the performance graphs at any time interval you deem necessary – even hourly if need be, and will receive certain alerts as to recommended actions to undertake to rectify things when the stats seem to take a dip. This way, you constantly stay on top of things and can only win.

Ambition is also particularly useful, as it incentivizes the individuals within the team to compete against each other and win.

LINKS FOR FURTHER INFORMATION

Sign up for training on a range of skills to improve your strategy: www.hellophoenix.wordpress.com/services/training

You may be pleasantly surprised that this link will soon redirect to the Academy of Social Sales; which is currently in the process of being established. Until such process is completed, you will enjoy my personal attention.

FREE DOWNLOADS:

Having learned how to compile key documents to kick-start and monitor your digital strategy ... here's my personal free give-away to you: templates. Use these as guidelines for your unique situation, and amend however you see fit. Enjoy.

Social Media Reporting Template
www.hellophoenix.wordpress.com/media/resources

Digital Competitors Analysis Template
www.hellophoenix.wordpress.com/media/resources

It will be an excellent idea to be glued to my blog, with regular articles posted on points of key interest, and to maintain pace with the industry. Simply go to www.hellophoenix.wordpress.com/blog

ABOUT THE AUTHOR

Meet Phoenix Sheldon-Baker - Business Strategist and Author of this book. Some of his successes include the onboarding of Fortune 500 companies as strategic business partners to black empowered entities in South Africa.

A former ghost-writer of content and online voice for several blue chip and JSE-listed corporations serviced by a digital marketing agency, Phoenix applied his unique and common-sense skill-sets to the benefit of very happy clients.

Phoenix also spent the last five years immersed in digital marketing operations interfacing business with digital strategy. With an expert knowledge and grasp of business imperatives across a range of sectors including publishing, fashion, recruitment, telecommunications, mining, retail, construction, automotives, finance, management consulting, government, charities and more, Phoenix writes, speaks to and trains people on the use of social media in everyday business.

CONNECT WITH PHOENIX

 If you have enjoyed this book, I would be very grateful if you leave a review and rating for it on Amazon.

 **Websites**
www.hellophoenix.wordpress.com

 **Facebook** Phoenix Sheldon-Baker
www.facebook.com/phoenix.sheldonbaker

 **Twitter** @PhoenixSheldon
www.twitter.com/PhoenixSheldon

 **LinkedIn** Phoenix Sheldon-Baker
www.za.linkedin.com/in/phoenixsheldonbaker

 **YouTube** Phoenix Sheldon-Baker
www.youtube.com/channel/PhoenixSheldon

 **Instagram** phoenixsheldonbaker
www.instagram.com/phoenixsheldonbaker

 Email to book me for a talk
thephoenix@execs.com

OTHER BOOKS BY PHOENIX

If you loved Sun Tzu for the Digital Age (the Uncut version), you will find the following books of great interest too. Some of these titles have not yet been released due to temporary revisions. Please do sign up for a notification when they get officially released by subscribing to any of my social media pages or website blog.

Goal: 1,000 Billionaires in Africa by 2030

The growth trajectory of wealth in the highest echelons of our evolving global economy is about to undergo unprecedented transformation, bringing benefit to emerging economies and to the developing world. The wealth-vortex to be generated will have an upward pull as the establishment of a new structure of global wealth sets-in over the next 15-years. To be included in the future of such never before-imagined financial abundance, you need to be strategically positioned both in business and in your social sphere. The central focus of this book is that Africa can change the world significantly by focusing on its wealth drivers and networking the efforts of 1,000 Billionaires to make this possible – a large portion whom will be self-made African Billionaires by 2030. The book is a call to action for people focused on wealth creation and changing the world a million dollars at a time. This book is a must-have for any business person engaged with Africa.

Dawn of the African White

Post-apartheid South Africa is a model showcase to the global community of how racism is being transcended. The liberation of people's freedoms further entrenches the success of democracy as a political model. Beneath the surface of a fundamentally changed socio-political landscape though, lurks an evil monster that periodically raises its head amongst liberated citizens accusing each other of past hatreds and being present culprits of affairs within a presumably tight economy. White people especially stand accused by the black majority for ongoing inequality, privilege and unfairly monopolizing wealth and its resources. These perceptions have further generated white fears of the country turning into another Zimbabwe, and its children having no economic future. While exploring the realities behind these perceptions, the book challenges white people for practicing superficial visionary leadership as the true reason why the country is the way it is. Dawn of the African White calls for a transformation of white identity and way of thinking. The book is intended to generate public debate on the rise of white African visionary leadership to work in the national interests of a non-racial and prosperous Africa.

Just Klap It!

A tongue in cheek satirical book on people who spend their lives talking about greatness, success, and happiness; and who never reach these things. This book is a motivational text to drive people to action their own destinies. It offers true self-empowerment through self-enlightenment and self-decision to set aside all internal considerations blocking one from performing the needed actions to materialize their dreams. It deals with the concepts of dreams, visions, missions and purposes. A must read for any person desiring success and happiness in life.

www.ingramcontent.com/pod-product-compliance
Lightning Source LLC
Chambersburg PA
CBHW070248190526
45169CB00001B/335